Resource Guarding

in Dogs

Understanding with

Compassion

Sylvia Koczerzuk, CPDT, CDBC

Disclaimer

The information provided in this book is intended for educational purposes only and is not a substitute for professional advice. Every dog is unique, and behaviour modification, especially in cases involving resource guarding, should be approached with care. While the techniques and methods shared in this book are designed to be effective and humane, the author cannot guarantee specific results as outcomes may vary depending on individual dogs, their environment, and how the advice is implemented.

It is highly recommended that dog guardians seek guidance from a certified professional dog trainer, certified dog behaviour consultant, or a veterinarian who has a specialty in up-to-date behaviour modification, especially in cases of severe aggression, fear-based behaviours, or if the safety of family members, other pets, or the public is at risk. The author and publisher deny any liability for damages, injuries, or other consequences that may result from the use or misuse of the information contained in this book.

Always prioritize safety, and never put yourself or others at risk when working with a dog exhibiting resource guarding or other potentially dangerous behaviours

About the Author

Sylvia Koczerzuk

Certified Dog Behaviour Consultant, Certified Pet Dog Trainer, Certified Separation Anxiety Trainer, Fear Free Certified Professional, Dynamic Dog Practitioner

Sylvia Koczerzuk is an experienced dog training and behaviour specialist with over 30 years in the pet care industry. Based in Kingsville, Ontario, she is the owner and founder of Walkabout Canine Consulting.

Sylvia's approach combines science-based training with a deep commitment to fear-free, compassionate methods— fostering positive relationships between dogs and their guardians. She holds certifications in pet dog training, separation anxiety training, and behaviour consulting, along with specialized expertise in posture and gait analysis as a *Dynamic Dog Practitioner.*

As a respected mentor and educator, Sylvia thrives on helping dog guardians understand complex behaviour issues through practical, empathetic solutions, from reactivity to resource guarding. Her programs emphasize calmness, engagement, and building resilience to create meaningful change. She is passionate about transforming the lives of dogs and their families, empowering owners with skills for confident, positive training experiences. Sylvia is dedicated to enriching the dog training community through education, collaboration, and mentorship

Dedicated to the dogs who have taught me more than any textbook ever could, and to the guardians and professionals walking the compassionate path of behaviour change.

Contents

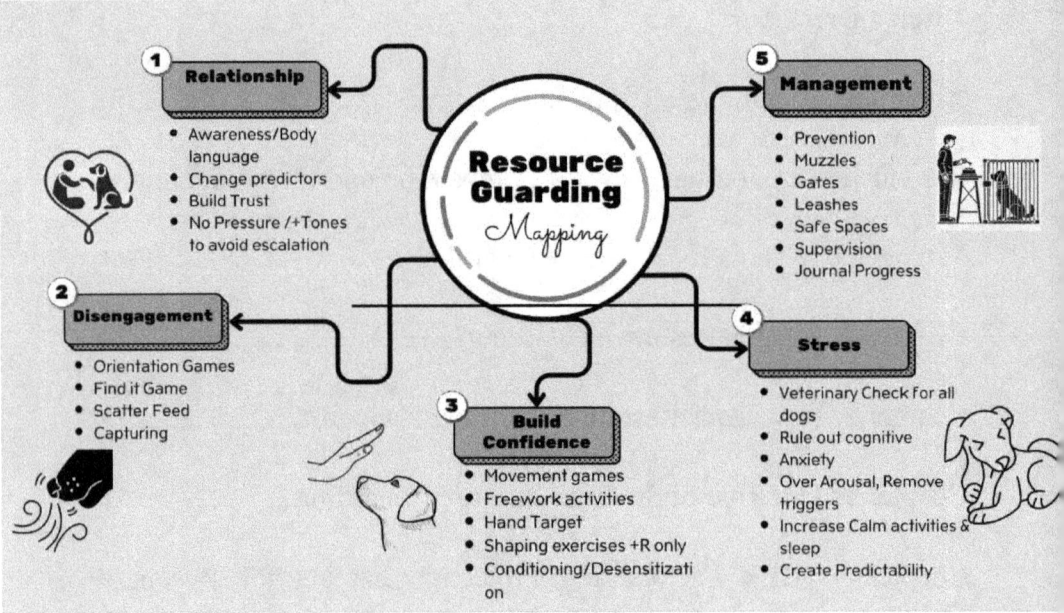

Introduction: A Journey Toward Compassion and Understanding

Dogs bring joy, companionship, and unconditional love into our lives, yet they also come with unique challenges. As a dog behaviour consultant with over 30 years of experience, I've worked with countless guardians and their beloved companions. One of the most common—and often misunderstood—issues I encounter is resource guarding.

This behaviour can be perplexing, even alarming, for dog owners. Why does your otherwise sweet and loving dog suddenly growl or snap over a bone, a toy, or even a comfy spot on the couch? It's easy to misinterpret this behaviour as defiance or aggression. But here's the truth: resource guarding isn't a sign of a "bad" dog—it's a natural response driven by fear, survival instincts, and sometimes even learned behaviour.

Through this book, I want to guide you on a journey of understanding. Together, we'll explore:

- *What resource guarding really is.*
- *The factors—biological, emotional, and environmental—that contribute to it.*
- *Practical, force-free strategies to manage and modify the behaviour.*
- *How compassion and understanding can transform your relationship with your dog.*

Whether you're a new dog guardian, a seasoned owner facing a sudden challenge, or a trainer seeking deeper insights into resource guarding, this book is for you. My goal is to help you see the world through your dog's eyes, empowering you with knowledge and tools to approach this issue with patience and empathy.

Above all, this book is about compassion—for your dog and for yourself. *Resource guarding* can be stressful, but it is also an opportunity to build trust, foster calmness, and deepen the bond with your canine companion. You'll find that the solutions are not just about stopping the behaviour but about creating a life where your dog feels safe, secure, and loved.

In my work, I've seen the transformative power of positive training and the joy it brings to both dogs and their families. I invite you to take the first step toward understanding and improving your dog's life—and yours. Together, let's turn challenges into opportunities and create a brighter, calmer future for you and your best friend.

Warmly,

Sylvia Koczerzuk

Management Tools for Resource Guarding

This section provides a foundational toolkit for managing resource guarding in dogs. Management tools are essential for ensuring safety, reducing stress, and setting the stage for successful behaviour modification. While training addresses the root causes of guarding behaviours, effective management prevents conflicts and creates a structured environment that fosters trust and calmness. From safe zones to enrichment toys, muzzles, leashes, and harnesses, these tools empower you to navigate challenging situations confidently and compassionately. By implementing the strategies outlined here, you can build a safer and more harmonious relationship with your dog as you work toward long-term solutions.

Muzzle Training for Safety in Resource Guarding

When addressing resource guarding in adult dogs, ensuring the safety of everyone involved—including the dog—is paramount. If your dog is displaying behaviours such as snapping, growling, or biting, muzzle training can be invaluable in creating a safe environment while you work on behaviour modification.

Why Muzzle Training is Important

A well-fitted, comfortable muzzle can prevent injuries and allow you to work with your dog more confidently. Muzzle training is not about punishment but safety. It provides the space to build trust and improve behaviour. A muzzle protects both your dog and those around them, enabling you to focus on training without fear of escalation.

Key Considerations for Muzzle Training

- **Muzzle as a Neutral Tool:** A *muzzle* should never predict something unpleasant for your dog. It should be introduced gradually and positively, using treats and rewards to create a neutral or even positive association.
- **Comfort and Fit:** Choose a muzzle that fits your dog comfortably. It should allow panting, drinking water, and taking treats. Selecting the right type and size is essential, and resources like MuzzleUp Project provide helpful guides, videos, and sizing tools to assist you.
- **Avoid Predicting Negative Experiences:** Do not use the muzzle during high-stress situations only, such as visits to the vet or grooming. Instead, incorporate it into regular, low-stress activities, such as walks or training sessions, to prevent your dog from associating the muzzle with negative events.

Steps to Introduce a Muzzle

1. **Show the Muzzle:** Allow your dog to sniff and explore the muzzle while rewarding them with treats. It creates a positive first impression.

2. **Pair the Muzzle with Treats:** Gradually encourage your dog to place their nose into the muzzle, using high-value treats. Avoid forcing it onto their face.

3. **Increase Duration:** Once your dog is comfortable placing their nose into the muzzle, practise securing it briefly, always rewarding your dog generously.

4. **Generalize the Muzzle:** Use the muzzle during calm activities like short walks or playtime. Keep the sessions short and enjoyable.

5. **Monitor Stress:** Watch for signs of discomfort or stress and adjust your approach as needed.

When to Use a Muzzle

Muzzles should only be used as a temporary safety tool during training sessions or when managing situations that may provoke guarding behaviours. They should not replace training or be used as a punishment. By ensuring the muzzle doesn't become a cue for negative events, you can prevent adding unnecessary stress to your dog's life.

Additional Resources

For more guidance on muzzle training, visit the MuzzleUp Project website, which offers detailed information, step-by-step videos, and tips for choosing the right muzzle for your dog.

Safe Zones and Management Spaces

Creating *safe zones* or *management spaces* is one of the most effective strategies for managing resource-guarding behaviours. These designated areas provide your dog with a secure, private space where they can feel safe with their valued items, free from the perceived threat of interference. By proactively setting up these spaces, you can prevent guarding incidents while reducing your dog's overall stress.

What Are Safe Zones?

Safe zones are designated areas where your dog can retreat to relax, eat, or enjoy high-value items without being disturbed. These spaces can include:

- **Crates:** An enclosed and private area that many dogs find calming when introduced properly.
- **Gated Areas:** Baby gates or exercise pens to section off parts of your home.
- **Rooms:** A quiet room or corner of your home dedicated to your dog's comfort and safety.

Why Safe Zones Work

Dogs often guard resources out of fear of losing them. Providing a safe zone removes the perceived threat, allowing your dog to feel secure and reducing the likelihood of guarding behaviours. Safe zones also help manage multi-dog households, preventing conflicts over resources.

Setting Up a Safe Zone

To create an effective safe zone:

1. **Choose the Right Location:** Pick a quiet area of your home where your dog can relax away from household traffic or noise.
2. **Make it Comfortable:** Add a soft bed, crate pad, or blanket. Include enrichment items like Kongs, Toppls, or chew toys to keep your dog occupied.
3. **Respect the Space:** Teach everyone in the household, including children, to leave the dog alone when they are in their safe zone. This is critical for maintaining your dog's trust in the space.

Using Safe Zones for Resource Guarding

Safe zones are particularly effective in these scenarios:

- **Meal Times:** Feed your dog in their safe zone to prevent guarding around food bowls. Remove any leftovers after they finish eating, wait until your dog leaves the area on its own, and leave the area alone to avoid future conflicts.

- **High-Value Items:** Allow your dog to enjoy chews, bones, or toys in their safe zone, ensuring they feel secure.

- **Managing Multi-Dog Households:** Use gates or separate rooms to prevent other pets from accessing a guarding dog's safe zone.

Using Dog Crates and Cots in Resource Guarding Management

Crates as Safe Zones

Crates can be invaluable tools in managing resource guarding, but their use should be carefully considered based on your dog's comfort and training history:

1. **For Crate-Trained Dogs**: If your dog is already crate-trained, the crate can serve as a safe, predictable environment where they can enjoy high-value items like chews or bones without feeling the need to guard. Ensure the crate is in a low-traffic area of your home, away from distractions, to create a sense of calm and security.

2. **For Non-Crate-Trained Dogs**: Introducing crate training during a period of high stress or behavioural management may not be ideal. For these dogs:

o   Assess whether crate training is a feasible step at this time or if it may add unnecessary stress.

o   Instead, consider other secure options like baby-gated rooms or exercise pens that provide a similar sense of safety without the need for crate training.

3. **Crate Alternatives**: If your dog has negative associations with crates, focus on creating other safe spaces using mats, beds, or designated quiet areas in the home using gates, as recommended above.

Dog Cots for Multi-Dog Households

In households with multiple dogs, dog *cots* can play a vital role in transferring the "safe space" concept:

1. **Portable Safe Zones**: Cots are easily movable and can extend the idea of a gated room to other parts of the house. This concept is particularly helpful when working on resource guarding in shared spaces or during family activities.

2. **Boundary Setting**: Teaching each dog to use their own cot helps create clear boundaries and reduces the likelihood of conflicts. You can use training techniques like the "Place" command to encourage dogs to settle on their cots.

3. **Shared Spaces**: For multi-dog households, clearly defined individual spaces—like cots—can help mitigate tension by

giving each dog their own "safe zone" that they are not expected to share.

Practical Steps for Implementing Crates or Cots

1. **Introduce Positively**: Ensure that both crates and cots are associated with positive experiences. Use treats, praise, or toys to encourage your dog to interact with these spaces.
2. **Practice Duration**: Gradually build up the amount of time your dog spends in their crate or on their cot, ensuring that the space remains a positive experience.
3. **Monitor Interactions**: In multi-dog households, supervise interactions to prevent one dog from encroaching on another's space, especially when high-value items are involved.
4. **Adapt for the Individual**: Every dog is unique. Consider their comfort level, past experiences, and current stress levels when deciding whether to use crates, cots, or other tools.

Introducing Your Dog to a Safe Zone

1. **Positive Associations:** Introduce the safe zone gradually, pairing it with treats, praise, and enrichment items to create a positive experience. Always leave your dog to experience the safety of this location without many interactions with it.

2. **Allow Choice:** Encourage your dog to enter the safe zone on their own rather than forcing them. Use cues like *"go to your bed"* or *"crate"* once the behaviour is established.

3. **Practice Regularly:** Incorporate the safe zone into your dog's daily routine. Encourage rest and downtime in the space, reinforcing calm behaviours.

Avoid Common Mistakes

- **Never Use the Safe Zone as Punishment:** Using the safe zone as a form of punishment can make the space aversive and counterproductive for reducing guarding behaviours.
- **Don't Disturb the Dog:** Ensure that no one approaches or interacts with the dog while they are in their safe zone, as this undermines the purpose of the space.
- **Supervise Early Stages:** Until your dog fully understands the purpose of the safe zone, monitor their interactions with the space to prevent stress or confusion.

Benefits of Safe Zones

Safe zones offer several benefits, including:

- Reduce your dog's stress and anxiety.
- Prevent guarding incidents before they happen.
- Create a predictable, structured environment for your dog.
- Foster independence and calmness.

By respecting your dog's need for a secure space and thoughtfully introducing safe zones, you can build trust and set the foundation for successful behaviour modification. Safe zones are not just a management tool—they are a vital part of creating a safe and peaceful home for everyone.

Leashes and Harnesses for Control

Leashes and harnesses are essential tools for safely managing your dog's behaviour during training and daily activities. These tools provide physical control, help prevent escalation of resource guarding or other challenging behaviours, and allow you to guide your dog effectively in potentially triggering situations.

When used appropriately, leashes and harnesses not only enhance safety but also foster a positive connection between you and your dog by creating clarity and reducing stress.

Why Leashes and Harnesses are Important

Leashes and harnesses serve as a physical connection between you and your dog, giving you the ability to:

- **Redirect Behaviour:** Safely guide your dog away from a guarded resource or trigger without escalating tension.
- **Prevent Access:** Stop your dog from approaching people, pets, or areas where guarding behaviours might occur.

- **Facilitate Training:** Maintain control during training exercises, helping your dog focus and engage with you rather than their surroundings.

Choosing the Right Equipment

1. **Leashes:**
   o **Standard Leashes (4-6 feet):** These are ideal for maintaining control during walks and training sessions. Avoid retractable leashes, as they can create inconsistent tension and reduce control.
   o **Long Lines (10-30 feet):** Useful for practicing recalls or allowing your dog freedom in controlled environments while maintaining safety.
2. **Harnesses:**
   o **Front-Clip Harnesses:** These are useful for managing pulling and allowing gentle redirection during training.
   o **Back-Clip Harnesses:** These are best for calmer dogs or those who do not pull, offering comfort and ease of movement.
   o **Dual-Clip Harnesses:** These provide versatility, with leash attachments at the front and back, offering more control options.
3. **Leash Accessories:**

- ○ **Traffic Handles:** Short loops attached near the base of the leash, providing extra control in high-stress situations.
- ○ **Carabiner Clips:** Useful for attaching to a second leash or anchor point in multi-dog scenarios.

Using Leashes and Harnesses for Resource Guarding

Leashes and harnesses are particularly helpful in managing resource-guarding behaviours, allowing you to:

- **Guide Your Dog Away:** Use the leash to calmly redirect your dog from a guarded item without confrontation.
- **Create Space:** Maintain a safe distance between your dog and potential triggers, such as people or other pets.
- **Support Training:** Incorporate leashes and harnesses into structured exercises, like boundary games or orientation games, to reinforce positive behaviours.

Training Tips for Effective Use

1. **Introduce the Tools Positively:** Ensure your dog associates the leash and harness with positive experiences by using treats and praise during the introduction.
2. **Maintain a Loose Leash:** Avoid constant tension on the leash, as it can increase stress or frustration.

3. **Pair with Verbal Cues:** Use cues like "let's go" or "leave it" alongside gentle leash guidance to communicate expectations.

4. **Practice Regularly:** Use the leash and harness during calm, low-pressure situations to build familiarity and confidence.

Case Example: Leash and Harness for Max's Guarding

Background: Max, a four-year-old German Shepherd, guarded his bed and growled if anyone approached. His guardian struggled to redirect him safely without escalating the situation. **Plan:** Max's guardian introduced a front-clip harness and a six-foot leash, which allowed her to gently guide him away from the bed while maintaining control. She paired leash guidance with a "let's go" cue and rewarded Max for moving away. **Outcome:** Over time, Max learned to disengage from guarding his bed, and his guardian felt more confident in handling similar situations.

Avoid Common Mistakes

- **Tugging or Jerking the Leash:** This can increase stress or create a negative association with the leash.
- **Using Inappropriate Equipment:** Avoid choke chains, prong collars, or other aversive tools that can harm your dog or escalate guarding behaviours.

- **Inconsistent Use:** Ensure everyone handling your dog uses the leash and harness consistently to avoid confusion.

Benefits of Leashes and Harnesses

When used effectively, leashes and harnesses:

- Provide safety and control in unpredictable situations.
- Help redirect your dog without confrontation or escalation.
- Support positive training and behaviour modification.
- Strengthen communication and trust between you and your dog.

Leashes and harnesses are more than just tools for control; they are integral to creating a safe and structured environment for your dog. By selecting the right equipment and using it thoughtfully, you can manage challenging behaviours while fostering a calm and positive relationship with your dog.

Interactive Enrichment to Redirect Guarding Behaviours

Enrichment is a powerful tool for redirecting resource-guarding behaviours and providing mental and physical stimulation. When introduced thoughtfully, interactive enrichment toys can help satisfy your dog's natural instincts, reducing their focus on guarding and redirecting their energy toward positive, engaging activities.

When using enrichment toys with dogs who guard, it's crucial to carefully consider how and when to offer these items to ensure safety and success.

Benefits of Interactive Enrichment

Interactive enrichment toys can:

- **Redirect Attention:** Shift your dog's focus away from guarding a specific resource to engaging in a mentally stimulating activity.
- **Reduce Stress:** Activities like foraging, licking, and chewing have a calming effect, helping lower arousal and stress levels.
- **Build Confidence:** Enrichment encourages problem-solving and exploration, which can help build your dog's overall confidence.
- **Provide a Positive Outlet:** Satisfy natural instincts like chewing, hunting, and foraging in a safe and controlled way.

Choosing the Right Enrichment Toys

When selecting enrichment items for dogs who guard, consider the following:

1. **Non-Guarded Items:** Choose toys that your dog has shown no history of guarding. Initially, avoid using highly valued items like rawhides or high-value chews.

2. **Safe Materials:** Select durable, non-toxic toys suited to your dog's chewing style and size.

3. **Ease of Use:** Start with toys that are easy for your dog to figure out, gradually increasing the challenge as they gain confidence.

Popular enrichment toys include:

- **Food Dispensing Toys:** Kongs, Toppls, and puzzle feeders. There are many do-it-yourself plans you can incorporate.
- **Licking Tools:** Lick mats or silicone baking mats spread with dog-safe treats like peanut butter or yogurt.
- **Foraging Games:** Snuffle mats or hide treats around the room for a "find it" game.
- **Chew Toys:** Long-lasting chews made from rubber or nylon, as long as these items aren't triggers for guarding.

Introducing Enrichment Toys to Guarding Dogs

For dogs prone to resource guarding, follow these steps to safely introduce enrichment toys:

1. **Set Up a Safe Zone:** Offer the toy in a designated safe zone, such as a crate, gated area, or quiet room. This ensures your dog can engage with the toy undisturbed.

2. **Start with Low-Value Fillings:** Begin with less enticing fillings or rewards to gauge your dog's comfort level. For

example, use kibble instead of high-value treats like cheese or peanut butter.

3. **Supervise Initially:** Observe your dog's interaction with the toy to ensure they remain relaxed and don't start guarding the item.

4. **Gradually Increase Value:** Once your dog is comfortable, introduce higher-value fillings or more challenging toys to keep them engaged.

5. **Rotate Toys:** Avoid leaving enrichment items out constantly. Rotating toys prevents them from becoming overly coveted and keeps them novel and exciting.

Case Example: Enrichment to Redirect Charlie's Guarding

Background: Charlie, a two-year-old Border Collie, guarded his food bowl and would growl when approached during meal times. His guardian wanted to reduce guarding while giving him an outlet for his energy.

Plan: Charlie's guardian started using a Kong with frozen kibble and low-sodium broth, offering it in his safe zone during quiet times. Initially, she supervised to ensure Charlie didn't display guarding behaviours. Over time, she increased the challenge by adding peanut butter and gradually moved the Kong into a more neutral area.

Outcome: Charlie became more focused on engaging with his Kong and less concerned about guarding his food bowl. His enrichment routine also reduced his overall stress.

Avoid Common Mistakes

- **Introducing High-Value Items Too Soon:** Start with lower-value rewards to build trust and reduce the risk of guarding.
- **Forcing Interaction:** Let your dog explore enrichment items at their own pace; avoid forcing them to engage.
- **Ignoring Guarding Signs:** If your dog shows signs of guarding (e.g., stiffening, growling), stop the session and reassess the value of the item or location.

Enrichment as a Long-Term Solution

Interactive enrichment is not just a management tool— it's a lifestyle enhancement for your dog. When incorporated thoughtfully, enrichment:

- Provides mental stimulation and reduces boredom.
- Builds positive associations with non-guarding behaviours.
- Offers a safe and enjoyable way to redirect guarding tendencies.

By making enrichment a consistent part of your dog's daily routine, you can create a more balanced and happier environment for both you and your canine companion.

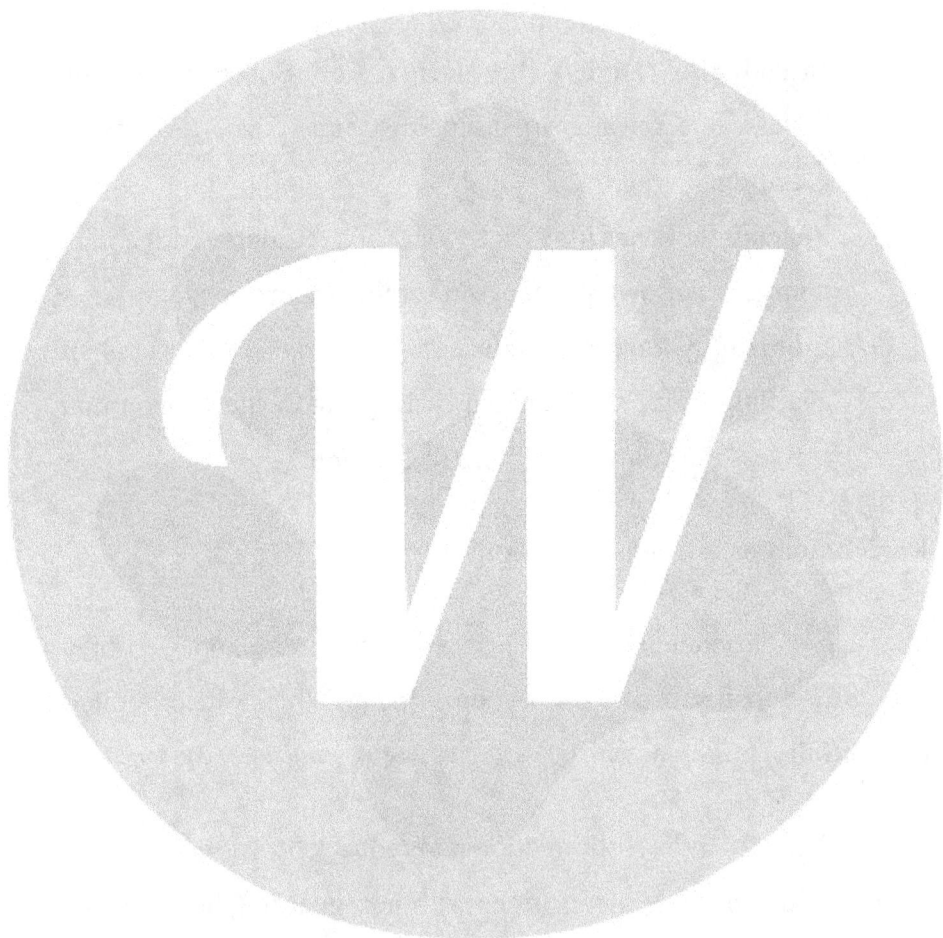

Chapter 1: What is Resource Guarding?

Resource guarding is a common, instinctual behaviour in dogs where they become possessive or defensive over certain items, spaces, or even people. While this behaviour can be unsettling for owners, it is deeply rooted in a dog's natural survival instincts. Understanding the diverse ways resource guarding presents itself is the first step in addressing and managing it.

Resource guarding is a natural behaviour in dogs that many owners encounter at some point. It occurs when a dog becomes **possessive** or **defensive** over certain items, spaces, or even people, preventing others—whether human or canine—from approaching what they value. While this behaviour can be confusing or alarming for dog owners, it is important to understand that resource-guarding is **instinctual** and rooted in survival.

Defining Resource Guarding

At its core, resource guarding is a dog's way of communicating that something they value is **off-limits** to others. Whether it is food, a toy, or a resting spot, the dog will display behaviours to **protect their resource**, making it clear that they do not want anyone—human or animal—coming near it.

Why Resource Guarding Happens

To understand why dogs guard resources, we must look at their ancestral roots. Dogs evolved from wild canines that often had to compete for food, territory, and safety. In the wild, failing to guard resources could mean **losing access to survival essentials**—whether food for sustenance or a secure place to rest.

This behaviour has been passed down through generations and is still **hard-wired** in dogs today. Even though domesticated dogs no longer need to fight for survival in the same way, they may still feel the **urge to protect** what they value most. This instinct is particularly strong in situations where:

- **Resources feel limited**: If a dog perceives that they may not have enough food or access to their favourite items, guarding behaviour becomes more likely.
- **The dog has a history of competition**: Dogs who have previously lived in situations where they had to compete for food or attention may be more prone to guarding.
- **The dog feels insecure**: Dogs that are anxious or unsure of their environment are more likely to protect what they feel is theirs.

What Resource Guarding Looks Like: Behavioural Signs

Resource guarding can manifest in a variety of ways, ranging from **subtle** signs that are easy to miss to more **overt** behaviours that are defensive or aggressive. These behaviours can be categorized into various levels of intensity, depending on how the dog perceives the threat to their resource.

Subtle Early Signs

In many cases, resource guarding begins with very subtle cues that owners may not even recognize as guarding. These early signs indicate the dog's growing discomfort or unease when others approach their valued resource.

- **Stillness**: Some dogs may be seen lying very quietly beside an object, appearing calm but highly alert.

- **Freezing**: The dog may suddenly stop moving or eating, becoming completely still when someone approaches. This stiff body posture is an early sign of discomfort.

- **Staring**: The dog might make direct, intense eye contact with anyone nearing the guarded resource. This is a warning signal that they are becoming defensive.

- **Whale Eye**: The whites of the dog's eyes become visible, often coupled with a sideways glance at the person or dog approaching the resource.

- **Lip Licking or Yawning**: *Displacement behaviours,* such as licking lips or yawning, are signs of mild stress that show the dog is uncomfortable with the situation.

Moderate Resource Guarding Behaviours

As the guarding behaviour escalates, the dog's warnings become more obvious. At this stage, the dog is more actively communicating that they want to be left alone with their resource:

- **Growling**: The dog may start to growl softly or loudly as a clear warning for others to stay away.

- **Showing Teeth**: Curling back the lips to reveal teeth is another defensive signal. This may go with growling or happen on its own as a more serious warning.

- **Positioning**: The dog may move to block access to the resource, using their body to physically prevent others from approaching. This may involve hovering over the item, standing stiffly beside it, or lying on top of it.

Severe Resource Guarding Behaviours

In more severe cases, resource guarding can escalate to defensive aggression if the dog perceives that their warnings have been ignored:

- **Snapping or Air Biting**: The dog may snap at the air or bite toward the approaching person or dog without making contact. This is a final effort to scare away the threat without causing harm.
- **Biting**: If all other warnings are ignored or if the dog feels cornered, they may resort to actual bites to protect their resource.
- **Lunging**: In extreme cases, the dog may lunge forward to assert dominance over the resource or create space between themselves and the perceived threat.

***CAUTION: If your dog is causing injury to you or other animals in the household, we urge you to reach out to a qualified behaviour consultant in your country. www.iaabc.org

Common Scenarios Where Resource Guarding Occurs

Resource guarding does not always happen with the same items or in the same way for every dog. The context in which it happens often depends on the **value** the dog assigns to the item or space, as well as their history with that resource. Here are some common scenarios where guarding may occur:

- **Food Guarding**: It is one of the most frequently seen forms of resource guarding. Food guarding can involve a dog becoming defensive over their meal, treats, bones, or even food they have stolen from the counter. Dogs may display the above guarding behaviours when someone comes near their food bowl or tries to take away a chew toy or bone.
- **Toy Guarding**: Many dogs guard toys they consider particularly valuable. This can range from a favourite ball or stuffed animal to random objects they have claimed as toys, such as socks or shoes. Toy guarding can be tricky because it often involves items the dog has found and sees as their prize.
- **Space Guarding**: Dogs may also guard their favourite resting spots, like a bed, crate, or even the couch. Space guarding can be more challenging to spot because the dog may appear calm when resting but grow defensive when approached.
- **Person Guarding (Owner Guarding)**: Some dogs guard their favourite person, becoming possessive when other dogs

or even people come near. This can be particularly problematic in multi-dog households or when new family members or visitors are introduced.

- **Found Items**: Dogs will sometimes guard items they have found or stolen, such as socks, shoes, or garbage. Even though these items may have little value, the dog perceives them as something worth protecting, making these situations difficult to manage. Humans can inadvertently make these situations more challenging by creating intense excitement around the item, such as chasing the dog, scolding them, or making dramatic attempts to retrieve the item. This can heighten the dog's perception of the item's value and reinforce guarding behaviour. Instead, remaining calm and using positive strategies to redirect the dog's attention can help diffuse the situation.

Identifying Guarding Behaviour Early

Recognizing resource guarding early on allows owners to intervene before the behaviour becomes more severe. By paying attention to the subtle signs—like freezing, staring, or lip licking—owners can start working on **management and training** strategies before the behaviour escalates into more serious defensive actions.

In the next chapter, we will explore **why** resource guarding happens and the underlying factors that contribute to it. Understanding the causes behind this behaviour will help you better prevent and manage it in your own dog.

Resource Guarding vs. Dominance

One common misconception is that resource guarding is about dominance. Many people believe that when a dog guards a resource, they are trying to "dominate" their owner or assert control, but this is not the case.

Resource guarding is about frustration, fear, and insecurity, and not control. The dog is not trying to be the boss; they are simply acting on an instinct to protect something valuable. In fact, trying to address resource guarding with dominance-based training methods—such as taking items away forcefully—can make the problem worse. The more a dog feels that their resources are being threatened, the more they will guard them.

To better understand this, think about how we, as humans, "resource guard." We lock the doors to our house and car, put fences around our yards, and secure valuables to protect them. How would you feel if someone were to walk into your home or take your car without permission? You would likely become frustrated, fearful, or even defensive. These actions aren't about asserting dominance but about maintaining security and peace of mind. Similarly, a dog is not trying to be "in charge"—they are simply trying to protect what they feel is important to them at that moment.

Common Misunderstandings

Owners often do not realize that guarding behaviours can be triggered by things beyond food or toys. A dog may guard spaces, like a favourite resting spot, or even their human companions. It is important to recognize that resource guarding is a broad behaviour that can present itself in many ways.

We may find it confusing or even illogical what dogs choose to guard or where these behaviours occur. However, it's crucial to understand that these actions make perfect sense in the dog's brain. Resource guarding stems from their perspective of value, security, and past experiences, even if it doesn't align with our human logic. Observing the patterns and trends in your dog's guarding behaviour can provide insight into their triggers and emotional needs, helping to create strategies that address the root cause rather than just the symptom.

For example:

- A dog may guard a particular **place**, like their bed or crate, by preventing others from approaching it.
- Some dogs exhibit **owner guarding**, where they become protective over their human family members, preventing other dogs or people from interacting with them.
- **Stolen items**, like socks or shoes, can also become guarded if the dog perceives them as valuable.

Next Steps: Understanding Your Dog's Unique Triggers

Resource guarding does not happen in a vacuum. Each dog is unique, and understanding the **specific triggers** that cause your dog to guard certain items or spaces is essential for effective management. In the next chapters, we will explore the various reasons behind resource guarding, how to prevent it from starting in puppies, and how to manage it effectively in adult dogs.

The Wildfire Effect: Why Early Intervention Matters

Resource guarding, if not addressed early, can quickly spread and intensify. What may start as a dog guarding food or a favourite toy can escalate to guarding random objects, spaces, or even people. This "wildfire effect" means that the more a dog practices guarding, the more ingrained and widespread the behaviour becomes. The broader the guarding tendencies grow, the harder they are to modify. When we are unable to predict what might be guarded next, it can create an unpredictable and potentially dangerous situation. This is why identifying patterns early and working towards solutions is so important.

Early intervention is essential to prevent this escalation. Without prompt guidance, a dog may start guarding newly encountered items—socks, shoes, or other everyday objects—simply due to a perceived or habitual value. Addressing guarding behaviours as soon as they appear can prevent this wildfire effect, keeping training manageable and the behaviour easier to change.

Case Study 1: A 12-Week-Old Retriever Puppy and Resource Guarding at the Vet

Background

I had been working with a wonderful client and her 12-week-old retriever-type puppy on foundational life skills. The puppy was well-bred and came from a reputable breeder, and the owner was dedicated to training. The dog displayed typical puppy behaviour— playful, curious, and eager to learn.

During one of our breaks between sessions, I received an email from the owner. She was very upset because her puppy had started to exhibit resource-guarding behaviour. This came as a shock, as everything had been progressing smoothly.

The Trigger

The incident occurred during a visit to the vet. The owner had brought along a chew toy to keep her puppy occupied. While the puppy was enjoying the chew, the veterinarian decided to take it away. The puppy growled in response. The vet then advised the owner to address the behaviour immediately by regularly taking things away from the puppy and "trading" for them.

Unfortunately, the recommended approach made things worse. The puppy began to guard resources more frequently and with greater intensity. This was a clear example of how an inappropriate approach can exacerbate the issue.

The Plan

When the client approached me, I reassured her that the situation was manageable and offered a tailored plan to address the resource guarding. The key points of the intervention included

1. **Avoiding Overuse of Trades**

   While trading items is often suggested for resource guarding, overusing this strategy can lead to frustration, particularly for retriever-type breeds. These dogs are genetically predisposed to carry objects in their mouths, and frequent removal of items can feel unnatural and stressful for them. Instead, I suggested shifting the focus to **disengagement**

games and the **toy switch game**, both of which promote voluntary relinquishment without causing frustration.

2. **Teaching Disengagement**

Disengagement is a critical skill for all dogs, especially those prone to guarding. Since the puppy was still young and learning, we started with simple exercises:

- o **Approach and Reward:** I recommended that the owner approach the puppy while he was eating or chewing, then drop something of higher value—like boiled chicken—near him. Over time, this helped the puppy associate the human approach with positive outcomes rather than fearing resource loss.

- o **Building the Behaviour:** The goal was to see the puppy naturally lift his head or stop chewing as the owner approached. This indicated a shift in the puppy's mindset from guarding to anticipating a reward.

3. **Classical Conditioning with "Drop" or "Not for You"**

We introduced a cue like "drop" or "not for you," paired with the action of dropping treats. This created a positive association with the verbal cue, helping the puppy understand that giving up an item would lead to a better outcome.

4. **Respecting the Puppy's Chews**

I emphasized the importance of allowing the puppy to enjoy his chews without interruption. Rather than removing the item while he was using it, the owner was instructed to wait until the puppy walked away. At that point, she could safely pick up the chew and even leave a small treat in its place as a reward for voluntary relinquishment.

Outcome

Within a few weeks of implementing these strategies, the puppy's resource guarding diminished significantly. The owner reported that her puppy no longer growled during approach and would even voluntarily offer his chew when cued. A combination of disengagement exercises, classical conditioning, and respect for the puppy's natural instincts successfully resolved the issue without causing additional stress.

Reflection

This case highlights the importance of understanding the individual dog's genetics and behaviour when addressing resource guarding. Retriever breeds, in particular, are predisposed to carry items, and taking things away repeatedly can lead to unnecessary frustration and guarding behaviours.

By focusing on building trust, teaching disengagement, and respecting the puppy's natural inclinations, we were able to transform a potentially concerning behaviour into a teachable moment that strengthened the bond between the dog and his owner.

Chapter 1: What is Resource Guarding?

Summary:

- **Definition**: Resource guarding is a natural, instinctual behaviour where a dog defends valued items, spaces, or people.
- **Why it Happens**: This behaviour is rooted in survival instincts and competition for resources in ancestral environments.
- **Early Warning Signs**: Subtle cues include stillness, freezing, intense staring, or lip licking.
- **Levels of Guarding**: Behaviours range from subtle cues to severe guarding behaviours, such as snapping or biting.

Checklist:

- Recognize early signs of guarding in your dog.
- Understand that resource guarding is about protection, not dominance.
- Name the items or situations your dog is guarding.

Chapter 2: How Does Resource Guarding Happen?

This chapter dives into the different causes of resource guarding, explaining the **natural instincts**, **emotional influences**, and **environmental factors** that drive this behaviour.

Resource guarding does not happen in a vacuum; it is not just a random behaviour that surfaces in certain dogs. Resource guarding is a deeply **instinctual behaviour** rooted in a dog's natural survival instincts. While it may seem problematic in the context of modern-day pet ownership, it is important to remember that this behaviour has evolved for a reason. In this chapter, we will explore the key reasons **why** resource guarding occurs and the many factors that can contribute to it.

Instinctual Survival Behaviour

At its core, resource guarding is about **survival**. In the wild, a dog's ancestors had to compete for resources—whether it was food, shelter, or mates—to survive. If an animal was not successful in securing these critical resources, they risked starvation, vulnerability, or even death. Over time, dogs evolved to develop strong protective instincts around things they valued, especially when those resources were scarce or contested.

While your pet dog does not need to fight for survival in the same way, these **survival instincts** are still deeply ingrained in their behaviour. When your dog guards something, they mean to say, "This is mine, and I need to protect it." They may not be guarding out of necessity, but their brain still triggers the instinct to secure what they perceive as important.

Competition for Resources

Competition for resources is another major driver of resource guarding. Dogs that have experienced **competition for food, toys, or attention**—especially during their formative months—are more likely to develop guarding behaviours. This can happen in a variety of situations:

- **Multi-Dog Households**: Dogs that grow up in homes with multiple dogs often must compete for food, toys, and human attention. If resources are limited, a dog may guard them to ensure they are not taken away.

- **Litter Competition**: Puppies who must compete for food or space with their littermates may be more likely to develop resource-guarding behaviours as they grow older. This is especially true if the competition is fierce or the puppy feels disadvantaged in their litter (e.g., smaller, weaker, or sickly puppies are likely to exhibit this behaviour).

- **Early Life Experiences**: Dogs that have spent time in shelters or foster homes where resources were scarce or inconsistent may develop guarding behaviours later in life. Dogs who have lived on the street and have not had access to food and/ or water. These dogs often feel insecure about whether they will have access to enough food or items, leading them to protect what they get. **(See Chapter 11, Addressing Resource Guarding in Rescue Dogs)**

Even in homes where competition is minimal, some dogs may still feel the urge to **protect** their resources, especially if they have learned that items can be taken away at any moment.

Stress and Insecurity

In many cases, resource guarding is linked to **stress** and **insecurity**. Dogs that are anxious, fearful, or uncertain about their environment are more likely to engage in guarding behaviours to feel more in control. When a dog feels like their environment is unpredictable or that they do not have access to enough resources, their natural response may be to guard the things they value most.

The **stress bucket** model is a helpful way to understand this. Every dog has a stress bucket—a metaphor for how much stress they can manage before they become overwhelmed. When a dog's stress bucket is nearly overflowing, they are more likely to show guarding behaviours.

Factors that fill the stress bucket can include:

- **Environmental Changes**: A change in routine, a new pet or baby in the home, or moving to a new house can all contribute to stress.
- **Overstimulation**: Loud noises, lots of activity, or too much interaction can overwhelm a dog, making them more likely to guard their resources.
- **Physical Discomfort or Pain**: Dogs in pain or discomfort may be more defensive of their space or resources, even if they were not guarders before. Medical conditions like allergies, gut issues, osteoarthritis (OA), injuries, or other medical conditions can lead to guarding behaviours.

Emotional Influences and Pessimism

Dogs experience a wide range of emotions, and those emotions can have a significant impact on their behaviour. Dogs that are naturally more **pessimistic**—meaning they expect negative outcomes—are more likely to guard resources. A pessimistic dog may assume that others are going to take their valued items away, leading them to defend those items pre-emptively.

On the flip side, **optimistic** dogs—those who expect positive outcomes—are more likely to share or give up resources without much resistance. This is why training and behaviour modification techniques often focus on **boosting optimism** in dogs, teaching them that good things happen when they share or give up their resources.

Medical Conditions and Pain

Medical conditions, particularly those that cause chronic pain or discomfort, can also contribute to resource guarding. Dogs experiencing pain may be more likely to guard their space or resources because they feel more vulnerable. For example:

- **Osteoarthritis**: A study has shown that 40% of dogs between the ages of 8 months and 4 years suffer from osteoarthritis. This condition can cause discomfort and make dogs more defensive of their space or items.

- **Injuries or Soreness**: Dogs recovering from injuries may feel the need to protect themselves or their environment, leading to guarding behaviours.

- **Other Health Issues**: Gastrointestinal discomfort, allergies, or any chronic condition that causes pain or stress can make a dog more prone to resource guarding.

If your dog's guarding behaviour seems to have escalated suddenly, or if it is accompanied by other changes in behaviour, it is important to consult a veterinarian to rule out any underlying medical issues.

Learned Behaviour

Resource guarding can also be a **learned behaviour**. In some cases, dogs learn that guarding items gets them what they want: to be left alone with their resource. If a dog growls or snaps and the perceived threat (human or dog) backs off, they learn that guarding is an effective strategy for protecting their possessions.

Similarly, dogs may learn to guard if their resources are often taken away. If a dog has repeatedly had toys, bones, or food removed by their owner, it may develop a **pattern of guarding** in anticipation of losing the item. In these cases, the dog's guarding behaviour is a response to a history of **negative experiences** with resource removal.

The Role of Genetics and Breed

Some breeds are more prone to resource guarding due to their genetic makeup and the specific roles they were bred to perform. For example, **gun dogs**—such as retrievers and spaniels—are bred to pick up and carry items as part of their working role. These dogs have a natural instinct to retrieve, and when this instinct is **thwarted** through constant removal of items or repetitive trading for items of lesser value, it can lead to frustration and eventually to **resource guarding**.

Gun dogs are wired to pick up, hold, and carry things. When humans repeatedly take these items away without fostering their **natural retrieving instinct**, the dog may start to see the removal as a negative experience. This is particularly true when they are asked to trade for something they perceive as less valuable. Over time, the dog may develop guarding behaviours to protect what they value most, especially if their desire to carry and hold is constantly interrupted.

This issue is not limited to gun dogs only. **Other breeds** that have strong instincts for holding or guarding items, like certain working dogs or herding dogs, terriers may also be more prone to resource guarding if their natural behaviours are not **flourished** or respected. In these cases, it is important to teach the dog to retrieve or trade in a way that respects their instincts while preventing guarding behaviours from escalating.

While genetics can certainly play a role, it is important to remember that resource guarding can develop in **any breed**, depending on the dog's environment, past experiences, and how their natural instincts develop into exaggerated responses.

Resource guarding is often viewed as a behaviour that is shaped by a dog's environment and experiences. However, **genetics** can also play a significant role in deciding whether a dog is more likely to show guarding tendencies.

The Role of Genetics in Behaviour

Behaviour, like many aspects of a dog's temperament, is shaped by both **nature (genetics)** and **nurture (environment)**. While resource guarding is a natural behaviour for many dogs, some breeds may be more likely to display these tendencies due to their genetic background.

Nature vs. Nurture

- **Nature**: Genetics provide the foundation for certain behaviours, such as guarding or retrieving, which can be seen more prominently in some breeds than others. These inherited traits influence how dogs interact with their environment and may predispose them to resource guarding.
- **Nurture**: While genetics set the groundwork, a dog's environment, experiences, and training can **mitigate or amplify** these tendencies. A dog with a genetic

predisposition to guarding may never develop the behaviour if they are raised in a calm, positive environment where resources are abundant and competition is low.

Breeds and Resource Guarding: A Genetic Perspective

Certain breeds are more prone to guarding behaviours due to the roles they were originally bred for. Understanding your dog's breed-specific tendencies can offer valuable insight into why they may be more likely to guard certain items, spaces, or people.

Genetics vs. Environment: A Complex Interaction

While certain breeds may have a genetic predisposition to resource guarding, this behaviour is not **set in stone**. The interaction between genetics and environment is complex, and many dogs with guarding tendencies can be trained to overcome these behaviours when raised in a supportive, structured environment.

The Role of Early Intervention Early intervention, especially in **puppyhood**, can significantly reduce the likelihood of resource guarding. By addressing guarding tendencies early and creating a **predictable, positive environment**, you can work with your dog's genetics rather than against them.

Preventing Guarding in Genetically Prone Dogs

Understanding your dog's genetic background is key to preventing resource guarding. By providing **positive outlets** for your dog's natural instincts and using proactive management, you can reduce the chance of developing this tendency even in genetically predisposed dogs.

Fulfill their Natural Instincts

Dogs bred for specific purposes, like retrieving or herding, need **positive outlets** for their natural instincts. Not providing these outlets can lead to frustration and guarding behaviours.

- **Gun Dogs:** Retrievers are genetically wired to retrieve and carry objects. Regularly engaging them in games like 'fetch' not only meets this instinctual need but also reduces the frustration that can lead to resource guarding. Without outlets like fetch, these dogs may try to satisfy their carrying instinct by grabbing household items or counter-surfing. Structured retrieval games can channel their natural drives constructively, reducing the likelihood of guarding or frustration-based behaviours.

- **Herding Breeds and Resource Guarding:** Herding breeds have a strong drive to "work." Structured activities can help fulfill this instinct, reducing stress and potential guarding behaviours. Engaging them in tasks like agility, obedience, or scent work provides the mental and physical stimulation they need, channelling their energy into positive outlets.

- **Terriers**: Terriers' natural hunting drive plays a significant role in their behaviours around possessions and guarding. Originally bred to control small prey populations, terriers have a strong prey instinct, which manifests in behaviours like intense focus, digging, and chasing. These traits can translate into a desire to "claim" or guard resources, especially if their energy and instincts are not directed positively. Recognizing this drive is essential to prevent and manage resource-guarding tendencies. Engaging terriers in scent games, structured activities, and constructive play can satisfy their hunting instincts in safe, controlled ways, reducing the chances of guarding behaviour and fostering a balanced, contented dog.

- **Resource Guarding Across All Breeds:** Resource guarding can occur in any breed, from Cavapoos to Papillons and beyond. While some breeds may have stronger genetic tendencies contributing to guarding behaviours, any dog can display resource guarding based on individual experiences, environment, or training history. Recognizing that guarding behaviours are not exclusive to certain breeds is essential for understanding each dog as an individual and addressing guarding tendencies proactively.

Use Positive Reinforcement and Management

Positive reinforcement and proper management can help mitigate guarding tendencies regardless of a dog's breed or genetic predisposition.

- **High-Value Trades**: While trading should not be the go-to solution, it can help prevent frustration at the moment. Adding animation to make the trade fun and exciting can encourage dogs to willingly give up items. Using **equal or higher-value items** prevents them from feeling like they are losing something important.
- **Environmental Management**: Provide safe spaces for dogs prone to guarding, especially when giving them high-value items like bones or chews. Always ensure they have their own space where they can feel secure without the need to guard.

Genetics and Guarding: Moving Forward

Understanding genetics' role in resource guarding helps dog guardians better manage and prevent these behaviours. While genetics may set the stage for guarding, **positive training, environmental management, and fulfilling a dog's natural instincts** can significantly reduce the impact of these tendencies. With the right approach, even dogs with strong guarding instincts can learn to trust and share their resources.

Chapter 2: How does resource guarding happen?

Summary:

- **Survival Instinct**: Stems from a need to secure resources.

- **Environmental Factors**: Dogs with a history of competition or insecure environments are more prone to guarding.

- **Stress**: High-stress levels increase guarding tendencies, illustrated by the "stress bucket" concept.

- **Medical Conditions**: Pain and discomfort can intensify guarding behaviours.

- **Genetics**: Certain breeds may have higher guarding instincts.

Checklist:

- Assess your dog's environment and sources of stress.

- Monitor for signs of pain or discomfort that could contribute to guarding.

- Consider your dog's breed and genetic background.

Chapter 3: The Role of Stress in Resource Guarding

This chapter covers the critical relationship between **stress and resource guarding**, offering practical tools and strategies for reducing stress and helping dogs manage their emotional responses.

Stress is one of the most significant contributors to behavioural issues in dogs, and resource guarding is no exception. Dogs, like humans, experience a range of stressors that can affect their overall emotional state. Understanding how **stress** influences resource guarding is key to successfully changing this behaviour. In this chapter, we will explore the **stress bucket** concept, how various stressors accumulate, and practical techniques to help reduce stress, leading to a calmer, more relaxed dog.

The Stress Bucket Concept

The **stress bucket** is a metaphor used to describe how dogs (and humans) experience and manage stress. Picture a bucket that fills up as your dog experiences different stressors. Each stressful event or situation adds a little more water to the bucket. If too much stress accumulates and the bucket overflows, it can result in **undesirable behaviours**, like resource guarding.

Elements of the Stress Bucket

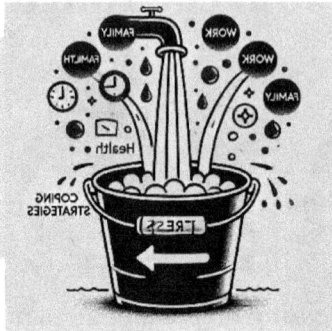

- **Size of the Bucket**: Every dog has a different ability to handle stress. Some dogs have a large bucket (high tolerance for stress), while others have a small bucket and can become overwhelmed more quickly.
- **What's Filling the Bucket**: Stressors can come from various sources, such as environmental changes, loud noises, new people or pets in the home, and lack of sleep or exercise.
- **The Hole at the Bottom of the Bucket**: This stands for how quickly a dog can recover from stress. Dogs with **good resilience** have a large hole that allows stress to drain quickly, while dogs with poor resilience may struggle to release stress, causing it to accumulate.

Stress and Resource Guarding

When a dog's stress bucket is full or overflowing, they are more likely to engage in **reactive behaviours**, such as resource-guarding. Stress not only triggers these behaviours but can also make it difficult for a dog to respond to training or behaviour modification techniques. A stressed dog is often **less capable of learning** or making good decisions because they are too focused on protecting themselves and their resources.

A. Chronic Stress: Dogs living with **chronic stress**, whether due to changes in the household, inconsistent routines, or fear-inducing events, are at a higher risk for developing or worsening resource-guarding behaviours. If a dog's bucket is constantly full, even small triggers, such as someone approaching their food bowl, can lead to a guarded response.

B. Stressors Leading to Resource Guarding: Common stressors that can contribute to resource guarding include:

- **New environments** (e.g., moving to a new home or adding new pets).
- Inconsistent or unpredictable routines.
- **Social stress** from other dogs, especially in multi-dog households.
- **Medical issues or pain** (such as osteoarthritis, which we discussed in earlier chapters).

- **Lack of rest** or too much excitement makes it hard for dogs to recover from daily activities.

Practical Techniques to Reduce Stress

The goal is to **reduce the amount of stress** accumulating in your dog's bucket, allowing them to feel more relaxed and less reactive. By addressing your dog's overall stress level, you can reduce the intensity of resource guarding and help them feel more secure.

A. Enrichment Activities to Reduce Stress

One of the best ways to reduce stress is by providing **mental and physical enrichment**. This helps dogs release pent-up energy, promotes calmness, and engages their minds in productive ways.

- **Scent Work**: Incorporating scent games, like the "Find It" game, can help **switch off** your dog's eyes and switch on their nose, leading to a more relaxed state.

- **Puzzle Toys and Kongs**: Giving your dog food puzzles or treat-dispensing toys can help them focus on problem-solving rather than guarding.

- **Free Work**: Allowing your dog to explore an environment filled with different objects, surfaces, and scents at their own pace encourages them to **use their body and brain** without pressure.

B. Active Rest and Quiet Time:

Active rest refers to calm, controlled activities that allow your dog to rest and recover without complete inactivity. Incorporating regular periods of **quiet time** and **low-stimulation environments** helps prevent stress from building up.

- **Safe Zones**: Create a designated safe zone where your dog can retreat and relax without being disturbed. This could be a crate, a quiet room, or a bed in a low-traffic area of the house.

- **Calmness Protocols**: Reward your dog for moments of **calm behaviour** by reinforcing relaxation with a low-value treat (as mentioned in the "Feed and Leave" strategy). Over time, this teaches your dog that being calm is rewarding and helps them manage their stress more effectively.

C. Consistent Routines

Dogs thrive on predictability. Establishing a consistent daily routine helps lower your dog's baseline stress level by providing structure. Knowing what to expect and when allows your dog to feel more in control, reducing anxiety and the tendency to guard resources.

- **Mealtimes:** Feed your dog at regular times in the exact location every day. This helps them feel secure about their access to food and reduces competition in multi-dog homes.
- **Training and Walks:** Keep training sessions and walks consistent in terms of time and location. When your dog knows what is coming, they are less likely to experience spikes in stress.

While predictability is key, the opposite can also contribute to stress. If a routine becomes too rigid or overly predictable, dogs may become aroused or frustrated- when even minor deviations occur. Being aware of signs of arousal during these times can help you adjust. Creating some flexibility within your routine—such as varying the order of activities or occasionally introducing new experiences—can help your dog adapt to change more easily and prevent stress from building up.

Building Resilience Through Confidence-Building

Resilience is the ability to bounce back from stressful or challenging situations. When it comes to **resource guarding**, building your dog's resilience is a powerful tool that helps them recover more quickly from stressful events and increases their ability to manage future stressors. A key part of resilience-building is **confidence**. When dogs feel confident, they are less likely to feel the need to guard resources because they trust that their needs will be met and their environment is safe.

Confidence-building activities should be included in your dog's daily routine, particularly when working through behaviour modification plans like resource guarding. The more confident your dog becomes, the less they will feel the need to rely on **defensive behaviours** like guarding. Here is how you can help build your dog's confidence:

A. Gradual Exposure to Triggers (Desensitization)

One effective way to build confidence is by gradually exposing your dog to their **triggers**—the situations that typically cause them stress. Start by introducing these triggers at **low intensities** and reward your dog for its calm behaviour. As your dog becomes more comfortable, you can slowly increase the intensity of exposure.

For example, if your dog guard's food:

- Begin by approaching their food bowl from a **distance** while they eat.
- Drop a **high-value treat** near the bowl to create a positive association.

- Over time, decrease the distance and continue to reward calm, non-guarding behaviour.

This gradual process teaches your dog that they do not need to react defensively when approached during mealtimes, helping them build confidence around food.

B. Teach New Skills and Focus on Success

Teaching your dog new skills is a fantastic way to build their confidence and resilience. When dogs successfully learn new behaviours and are rewarded for them, their sense of control and accomplishment increases. This is especially important for dogs that tend to **guard resources**, as they may lack confidence in other areas of their life.

- **Target Training**: Teaching your dog to target their nose or paw to your hand is a wonderful way to **boost focus** and create an interactive, positive experience. This gives your dog an easy task to complete, which builds trust and confidence while reducing stress in challenging situations. You can further this training by asking your dog to touch their nose to different objects.
- **Clicker Training**: Using a **clicker** to mark and reward desired behaviours can quickly build confidence. Dogs learn that they can control their environment by offering certain behaviours and receiving rewards for them. This positive

reinforcement-based approach teaches them that **good things happen** when they engage cooperatively. Caution for noise-sensitive dogs or dogs who become compulsive: use verbal markers like "good," "yes," "super, "or "nice."

- **Success-Based Training**: Ensure that your dog experiences success during training. If your dog struggles with a task, lower the criteria so they can succeed, then gradually increase the difficulty as their confidence grows. Building on small successes will enhance your dog's ability to tackle more complex tasks over time. You can even start by just rewarding any behaviour that helps reduce pressure and encourages your dog's confidence.

C. Interactive Play and Problem-Solving Games

Engaging in interactive play and offering **problem-solving games** helps boost confidence by allowing dogs to use their natural problem-solving abilities and instincts. These activities engage their mind, providing positive outlets for energy while reducing feelings of frustration or fear.

- **Puzzle Toys and Food Enrichment**: Offering puzzle toys that require your dog to think and work to retrieve a reward is a fantastic way to **build problem-solving skills** and self-confidence. These toys challenge your dog in a productive way and reinforce the idea that *effort leads to success*.

- **Scent Work**: Allowing your dog to engage their **scenting abilities** is incredibly rewarding for them. Scent games, like hiding treats around the house or yard and encouraging your dog to find them, build confidence by tapping into their natural instincts. The sense of achievement they experience when they find the treat boosts their overall resilience and confidence.

- **Interactive Play**: Games like **tug** (when done appropriately) or **fetch** can be valuable confidence boosters if the games are **structured** and involve clear rules. Dogs that understand the boundaries of these games and who win or are rewarded for playing within the rules develop confidence in their interactions with humans.

D. Positive Reinforcement and Encouraging Independence

Building confidence in dogs, especially those prone to resource guarding, requires consistent use of **positive reinforcement**. Rewarding your dog for desired behaviours and offering plenty of opportunities to **make their own choices** (within safe boundaries) helps them feel empowered rather than anxious or defensive.

- **Choice-Based Training**: Give your dog the ability to make choices in non-guarding situations. For example, allow them to choose between two toys or decide when they want to retreat to their safe zone. Giving dogs control over certain decisions makes them feel more secure and reduces feelings of helplessness, which can fuel guarding behaviours.

- **Confidence in Solitude**: Encourage your dog to spend time independently, such as chewing on a toy or enjoying a treat in their safe space. Reward them for staying calm and relaxed when alone. Teaching your dog to enjoy solitary activities reduces their reliance on human attention or constant interaction, which can help diminish guarding behaviours over time.

E. Addressing Frustration and Impulse Control

Resource guarding often stems from **frustration** or a lack of **impulse control**. Teaching your dog to manage frustration and control their impulses is key to reducing guarding behaviours and building resilience. These exercises help dogs stay calm, even when they are excited or anxious.

- **Impulse Control Games**: Games like "**Wait for It**" or "**Leave It**" help dogs practice **self-control**. Start by asking your dog to wait for a treat or toy, rewarding them when they succeed. These games teach dogs that waiting calmly leads to good things, helping them manage their impulses and avoid impulsive guarding behaviours. Watch how your dogs respond to these games to decide whether they can enjoy the game, which is what positive training should always focus on.

- **Frustration Tolerance Exercises**: Dogs that guard may have a **low tolerance for frustration**, leading to defensive reactions. Building frustration tolerance involves gradually increasing the difficulty of tasks or challenges and rewarding your dog for sticking with it without becoming frustrated or reactive. Over time, they learn to handle frustration more gracefully.

F. Body Language and Communication

Learning to read and respond to your dog's **body language** is an essential part of building their confidence. When dogs feel understood and supported, their confidence increases, making them less likely to guard or react negatively.

- **Clear Signals**: Pay attention to subtle signs of stress, such as **lip licking**, **stiffness**, or **whale eye** (when the whites of their eyes are visible). Address these signs early by offering a break, engaging in a calming activity, or providing reassurance. The more you communicate clearly with your dog, the more they trust you in stressful situations.
- **Use of Bridging Cues**: Incorporate **bridging cues**, such as saying "good" or using a clicker, to signal your dog that they are on the right track. This consistent feedback helps dogs feel confident in their behaviour, reducing their anxiety and guarding tendencies.

Conclusion: Building a More Resilient Dog

Confidence-building is an integral part of managing and changing resource-guarding behaviours. By providing opportunities for **success, positive interactions, and skill-building**, you help your dog develop the **resilience** to handle stress without resorting to guarding. Whether through structured games, gradual exposure to stressors, or daily enrichment, these confidence-boosting activities will lead to a more secure, relaxed, and adaptable dog.

Signs of an Overflowing Stress Bucket

It is important to recognize when your dog's stress bucket is getting too full so you can intervene before resource guarding escalates. Look for these signs of stress:

- **Excessive panting** or drooling in non-stressful situations.
- **Restlessness** or inability to settle.
- **Hypervigilance**: They are constantly scanning their environment or reacting to slight changes.
- **Body stiffness** when other animals or people approach.
- **Excessive shedding**, paw licking, or other physical signs of stress.

By recognizing these signs early, you can help reduce stress before it turns into reactive behaviour like guarding.

Long-Term Stress Management

Managing stress is not a one-time fix. It requires **consistent attention** to your dog's emotional well-being. By continuously managing stress, using enrichment activities, and reinforcing calm behaviours, you can help your dog build resilience and reduce the likelihood of resource guarding over time.

- **Routine Check-Ins**: Make it a habit to regularly assess your dog's stress levels. Are there any new stressors? How is your dog reacting to daily routines? Consistently managing stress helps prevent it from accumulating and leading to unwanted behaviours.

Chapter 3: The Role of Stress in Resource Guarding

Summary:

- **Stress Bucket Concept**: Stress accumulates like water in a bucket; when it overflows, guarding behaviours can intensify.
- **Types of Stress**: Name stressors from environmental factors, health issues, or routines, and recognize signs of stress like excessive panting or stiffness.
- **Managing Stress**: Use routines, calmness protocols, and enrichment to reduce stress and build resilience.

Checklist:

- Monitor your dog for signs of stress.
- Use enrichment activities to help relieve stress.
- Create a predictable routine and safe spaces to reduce stress accumulation.

Chapter 4: Risk Factors and Protective Factors for Resource Guarding

This chapter covers key risk factors, protective strategies for preventing resource guarding, and actionable insights for dog guardians.

Resource guarding does not develop in every dog, but certain factors increase the likelihood of it occurring. By understanding these **risk factors**, dog owners and trainers can take steps to reduce or prevent resource guarding before it becomes a serious issue. Additionally, there are important **protective factors** that can help prevent the behaviour from escalating or even beginning in the first place.

Risk Factors: What Makes Resource Guarding More Likely?

Competition for Resources

One of the most significant risk factors for resource guarding is the **competition** a dog experiences for resources. Dogs that must compete with other animals—whether in their litter, shelter, or multi-dog household—are more likely to develop guarding behaviours. This competition creates an environment where a dog feels they must **secure their resources** to ensure access to them.

- **Multi-Dog Households**: In homes with multiple dogs, the competition for food, toys, and even human attention can drive resource guarding. Dogs who feel that they must fight for these resources are more likely to guard them.

- **Shelter and Rescue Dogs**: Dogs who have spent time in shelters, where resources like food and space may have been limited, are often more prone to guarding behaviours. The environment of scarcity makes them feel the need to protect what they get. We know now that when dogs are adopted and settled into their new home, resource guarding can resolve on its own as the shelter's stress factor is gone.

Early Experiences

Dogs' early experiences, particularly during their **critical socialization period** (around 3-14 weeks of age), play a key role in whether they develop resource guarding. Dogs not exposed to positive experiences with sharing or giving up resources during this stage are more likely to develop guarding tendencies later in life.

- **Negative Interactions**: Dogs that repeatedly have items taken away from them harshly or unexpectedly may learn to guard in response. This creates a pattern where the dog feels that they must protect their items to keep them.

Stress and Anxiety

Stress is a major contributing factor in resource guarding. Stressed or anxious dogs are more likely to show guarding behaviours as part of a broader struggle to feel **secure** in their environment. Stress can come from many sources, such as changes in routine, a lack of structure, training methods, new stressors in the home, or even **underlying medical conditions** that cause pain or discomfort.

- **Cumulative Stress**: Dogs with full or nearly full **stress buckets**—due to environmental factors, social stressors, or physical discomfort—are far more likely to guard their resources. When a dog's stress levels are consistently high, even minor triggers can cause a defensive response.

Genetics and Breed Tendencies:

As discussed in Chapter 2, **genetics can** affect a dog's likelihood to guard. Certain breeds, like gun dogs, may be more predisposed to resource-guarding due to their instinctual behaviours. Dogs that were bred to **retrieve, hold, or protect items** are more likely to guard if their natural instincts are thwarted. Also, if you have a dog breed that is not given the opportunity to do dog things, you can see this contributing to stress.

- **Gun Dogs**: Gun dogs, bred to retrieve and carry items, are often frustrated when their instinct to pick up and hold things is interrupted by the constant removal of items. This can lead to resource guarding if not managed properly.
- **Working and Herding Dogs**: Similarly, working dogs bred to guard or control items or territory may be more prone to developing guarding behaviours if their environment or management does not align with their instincts.

Medical Conditions

Pain or discomfort can also be a key driver of resource guarding. Dogs experiencing pain, whether from injuries, arthritis, or other health conditions, may feel the need to guard their space or items to avoid further discomfort or perceived threats.

- **Osteoarthritis:** A significant percentage of young dogs (8 months to 4 years) can start to suffer from osteoarthritis, which can cause guarding behaviours due to discomfort.
- **Other Health Issues:** Digestive issues, dental pain, or any underlying health condition affecting the dog's comfort level can increase the likelihood of guarding. These issues must be ruled out.

Case Study: A dog was observed to resource-guard their bed from their owners every afternoon after their daily walk. This behaviour was consistent and seemed to escalate despite several attempts to manage it. Upon assessment by a behaviour consultant, who carefully observed the dog's posture and gait, the guardians were advised to have the dog checked by a veterinarian. The evaluation revealed arthritis, and after starting the dog on appropriate pain medication, the resource-guarding behaviour disappeared completely. This case highlights the importance of investigating potential medical causes when addressing guarding behaviours.

Protective Factors: Reducing the Likelihood of Resource Guarding

While several factors can increase the risk of resource guarding, there are also protective factors that can help reduce the likelihood of guarding behaviours developing. These include:

Positive Early Socialization

One of the best ways to prevent resource guarding is through **positive early socialization**. During a dog's critical socialization period, exposing them to **various situations** where they learn that sharing or giving up resources does not lead to negative outcomes is important. Introducing puppies to controlled situations where they can experience trading items or interacting with other dogs around resources in a positive manner can help prevent guarding from developing.

- **Gradual Exposure**: Gradually introducing dogs to scenarios where they share or give up items and rewarding them for doing so can build trust and reduce the likelihood of guarding later.

Teaching Reliable Cues

Teaching dogs **reliable cues** such as "drop it" and "leave it" can function as powerful tools in preventing and managing resource guarding. These cues should be taught with **positive reinforcement** so the dog associates giving up or moving away from the item with something positive rather than losing out.

- **Positive Associations**: When dogs learn that giving up items or moving away from them results in a positive outcome— like receiving a high-value treat—they are more likely to relinquish resources willingly.

Fostering Optimism

Dogs that are **optimistic**—those who expect positive outcomes in their interactions—are less likely to guard resources. By building trust and creating **predictable** routines, dogs can develop confidence that they will not lose their valued resources.

- **Boosting Optimism**: Enrichment activities, games, and **positive reinforcement** training contribute to a dog's overall optimism. Dogs that feel secure in their environment are less likely to feel the need to guard.

Structured Management and Boundaries

Creating **safe spaces** and managing a dog's environment can reduce stress and the risk of resource guarding. Giving each dog their own space to eat, chew, and relax without feeling threatened by other dogs or people helps create a **predictable** and **stress-free** environment. Teaching everyone in the household to respect the dogs' safe spaces and eating time.

- **Gated Areas and Safe Zones**: Setting up gates or designated areas where dogs can enjoy their food or toys without interruption can prevent the feeling of needing to guard.
- **Predictable Routines**: Consistent routines around feeding, playing, and resting can help dogs feel more secure in their environment, reducing the likelihood of guarding behaviours.

Positive Reinforcement and Training

Using **positive reinforcement** techniques is key to preventing and managing resource guarding. Punishment or forceful removal of items can worsen guarding while rewarding positive behaviours—like willingly giving up an item—builds trust and reduces the need to guard.

The Role of Relationship in Resource Guarding: Building Trust and Predictability

One of the most important aspects of addressing **resource guarding** in dogs is the quality of the relationship between the dog and their guardian. A dog that feels secure, trusts its guardian, and understands what to expect is less likely to engage in defensive behaviours such as guarding. In contrast, dogs that experience **reprimands, inconsistency, or unpredictable handling** may develop stronger guarding tendencies to protect their resources and ensure their needs are met.

Positive Feedback vs. Reprimands

Using **positive reinforcement** and constructive feedback in training helps build a **trusting relationship** between the dog and the guardian. When dogs are consistently rewarded for desired behaviours and treated kindly, they begin to see their guardian as a source of **safety** and **good outcomes**.

How Positive Feedback Affects Resource Guarding:

- Dogs learn that **approaching their guardian** does not result in losing their valued resources but rather leads to something **better**—a treat, affection, or another positive experience.
- **Consistent positive feedback** reduces stress and anxiety, leading to a more secure and confident dog that feels less need to guard their resources.

- Trust is built over time when dogs can predict that their guardian will respond with kindness rather than with harsh reprimands or punishment.

In contrast, **reprimands and punishment** can damage the relationship, making the dog feel they need to guard their resources even more. The unpredictability of punishment can cause a dog to feel anxious and insecure, worsening guarding behaviours.

Building Trust and Predictability

Dogs thrive on **predictability**—knowing what to expect in their daily interactions. When dogs understand that their guardian will respond to guarding situations with **calmness and positivity**, they become less likely to feel threatened or defensive.

Ways to Build Trust and Predictability:

- **Consistent Routines**: Keep daily routines as predictable as possible. Feeding, walks, and playtime should happen around the same time each day, helping the dog feel secure in their environment.
- **Calm Approaches**: When approaching a dog who is guarding an item, do so calmly and without threat. Avoid sudden movements or taking the item by force. Instead, trade for a higher-value item or calmly distract the dog.
- **Positive Reinforcement**: Reinforce calm behaviours with treats and praise. If your dog is lying down near a guarded

item without showing guarding behaviour, acknowledge that moment with quiet praise or a food reward.

When dogs trust that their guardian will not suddenly take away resources or respond with punishment, they are more likely to **relax their guard** and allow others near their valued possessions.

Strengthening the Relationship Through Predictability and Positive Experiences

Resource guarding can often indicate that a dog is uncertain about their relationship with their guardian. Building a **positive, trusting bond** with your dog is one of the best ways to reduce resource-guarding behaviours. By ensuring that your interactions with your dog are **predictable, positive, and reinforcing**, you help build a foundation of trust.

Strategies to Strengthen Your Relationship:

- **Hand Feeding**: Using your dog's daily food allowance to hand-feed them can improve trust and build positive associations. Dogs learn that food comes directly from their guardian, reinforcing the idea that the guardian is a provider, not a threat.
- **Engage in Cooperative Games**: Play games like 'fetch,' 'tug,' or 'find it' with clear rules and rewards. These games teach your dog to cooperate and share resources in a

structured and predictable way, reinforcing positive behaviours.

- **No More "No's"**: Avoid excessive use of reprimands such as saying "no" or scolding. Instead, redirect behaviours you do not want by offering a more acceptable choice and rewarding the desired behaviour.

Over time, these positive experiences help your dog feel more secure, trusting, and confident in their relationship with you. They are less likely to guard resources because they **trust that their needs will be met** without conflict or loss.

Chapter 4: Risk and Protective Factors

Summary:

- **Risk Factors**: Early competition, negative experiences, stress, and genetics increase guarding risks.
- **Protective Factors**: Positive early socialization, teaching cues like "drop it," structured management, and fostering optimism.

Checklist:

- Create safe spaces where your dog can enjoy valued items undisturbed.
- Use "drop it" and "leave it" cues for routine training.
- Reinforce sharing behaviours with positive associations.

Chapter 5: Preventing Resource Guarding in Puppies

This chapter focuses on early intervention and training strategies to prevent resource guarding in puppies.

One of the best ways to address resource guarding is to **prevent it from developing in the first place**, especially in puppies. By taking a proactive approach to training, socialization, and management, we can set puppies up for success, helping them learn that sharing and giving up items leads to positive experiences. In this chapter, we will explore key strategies for preventing resource guarding in puppies and how to instill **healthy habits** that reduce the likelihood of guarding behaviour later in life.

Early Socialization: The Key to Prevention

The **early socialization period** (3 to 14 weeks) is a crucial time in a puppy's life for learning to interact with their environment and others. During this window, puppies are especially receptive to new experiences, which makes it the ideal time to teach **positive associations** around resources. Introducing puppies to different situations in a **controlled, positive way** can help prevent resource guarding from developing.

Sharing and Trading Games

One of the most effective ways to prevent resource guarding in puppies is through **sharing and trading games**. These games help puppies understand that giving up items or sharing them does not mean losing out.

- **Toy Switch Game**: The **Toy Switch** game is a splendid example of teaching puppies to drop and exchange items. Using two equally valuable toys, engage your puppy with one toy until they are interested. Then, switch to the second toy and play with that. Encourage them to drop the first toy by making the second one more interesting. This teaches puppies that giving up one toy leads to fun with another, which builds **trust and positive associations**.

- **High-Value Trades:** While trading is a quick and easy solution when a puppy has something they should not, it is important not to **rely heavily** on this technique for a long-term basis. Trading can help for the moment, but the goal should be to teach the puppy that giving up or sharing items is a positive experience without always needing to exchange one thing for another.

- One strategy that works especially well is to **add animation** and **excitement** when your puppy has something in their mouth. Instead of immediately offering a trade, show your puppy that you are **genuinely excited** about what they have. By creating a sense of joy and enthusiasm, you can make the puppy feel that what they have is **brilliant**, encouraging them to **share it with you** willingly.

- **How to Use Animation and Excitement**: When your puppy picks up an object, use a **happy tone** and show excitement about what they have found. Clap your hands, smile, and function as though the item is something incredible. This playful energy encourages your puppy to bring the item to you, turning the interaction into a **positive and shared experience**. Over time, the puppy learns that coming to you with items is fun and rewarding, which prevents guarding behaviour from developing.

By starting this process right from the beginning, you create a **positive association** between the puppy and sharing, ensuring they feel safe and excited to approach you with their valued items.

Exposure to Resource Sharing

Introducing puppies to **controlled resource-sharing scenarios** early in life is critical. Let them experience sharing toys or food in a safe and enjoyable way. Positive interactions with humans or other dogs while eating or playing will help puppies understand that there is no need to guard.

- **Supervised Feeding**: Feeding puppies in a calm, supervised environment where they feel safe helps reduce any fear associated with losing their food. During meals, drop a few pieces of **high-value food** into their bowl as they eat to reinforce the idea that good things happen when humans approach during mealtime.

Multi-Dog Homes and Resource Sharing

In homes with multiple dogs, it is important to **check how puppies interact** with the other dogs around resources. Provide **separate spaces** for each dog to enjoy food, toys, or chews to prevent competition and guarding behaviour from developing.

- **Designated Feeding Areas**: From the start, show designated feeding areas or "safe zones" where each dog can eat without interference. This ensures that the puppy does not feel threatened by competition for resources.

Teaching Key Cues Early

Teaching puppies essential cues like **"Leave it"** and **"Drop it"** early on can prevent guarding behaviours from taking root. When these cues are reinforced positively, puppies learn that relinquishing an item or disengaging from a resource results in a **reward** rather than the loss of something valuable.

Teaching "Drop It"

The cue "Drop it" is a valuable tool for preventing resource guarding. This command encourages the puppy to release whatever they are holding, knowing that something better is coming their way.

- **How to Teach It**: Start by giving your puppy a low-value toy or object. Once they have it in their mouth, offer a **high-value treat** while saying, "Drop it." As soon as they release the toy, give them the treat. Practice this in various contexts, gradually increasing the value of the items they are holding. The goal is for the puppy to learn that dropping an item results in a **positive outcome**.

Teaching "Leave It" The "Leave it" cue teaches puppies to disengage from an item before they even grab it. This cue can be particularly helpful in preventing future guarding issues, as it encourages the puppy to ignore objects they might otherwise become possessive over.

- **How to Teach It**: Hold a treat in your closed hand and let the puppy sniff or paw at it. Say "Leave it" and wait until the puppy disengages. As soon as they stop trying to get the treat, offer them a different treat from your other hand. This teaches them that **not engaging** with the item leads to a reward.

Case Study #4: 12-Week-Old French Bulldog

Overview

During a private life skills session with a 12-week-old French Bulldog, the owner raised concerns about the puppy picking up items he wasn't supposed to have and running away. While common in puppies, this behaviour can be frustrating for owners and may lead to resource guarding if mishandled.

Situation

The behaviour was observed during the session when the puppy picked up an item and ran off. The owner's instinct might have been to chase the puppy or sternly ask for the item back, but these approaches often backfire, reinforcing the puppy's enjoyment of the "game" or causing stress.

Intervention

I demonstrated an **in-the-moment handling technique:**

1. **Capturing Attention**: I clapped to create an attractive and novel sound. This immediately grabbed the puppy's attention, as puppies are naturally curious and responsive to unexpected stimuli.

2. **Engaging with Enthusiasm**: Using an exaggerated, happy tone, I acted as if the puppy's behaviour was the most exciting and wonderful thing:

   o "Oh my gosh! What do you have? That's so amazing! Wow, this is fantastic!"

   o My tone and energy communicated excitement, encouraging the puppy to approach me instead of running away.

3. **Reinforcing Trust**: When the puppy came to me to "show off" the item, I celebrated his decision to approach. This was crucial in building trust and avoiding feeling threatened or needing to guard the item.

4. **Prompt Item Drop**: The excitement and trust made it easy for the puppy to drop the item without coercion. At this moment, the puppy received a reward (treat or praise), reinforcing the positive experience.

Results

The puppy learned that bringing items to the owner instead of running away is more rewarding. The owner witnessed an immediate, stress-free solution and saw how tone, energy, and positive reinforcement could redirect unwanted behaviours.

Key Takeaways for Owners

1. **Avoid Chasing**: Chasing reinforces the "game" and may escalate guarding behaviour.
2. **Use Novel Stimuli**: A sudden sound like clapping can effectively grab attention.
3. **Celebrate the Puppy's Choice**: Show genuine excitement to encourage the puppy to approach.
4. **Reward Desired Behaviour**: Always reward the puppy for coming to you and dropping the item.

Owner Homework

1. Practice this approach whenever the puppy picks up something inappropriate.
2. Use high-value rewards to strengthen the positive association.
3. Introduce a trade game by exchanging the item for a treat or a toy of equal or greater value.

Conclusion

This experience demonstrates the importance of using positive, in-the-moment techniques to manage behaviours effectively and prevent future issues like resource guarding. The French Bulldog puppy responded beautifully, showcasing the power of engagement and trust-building.

Managing the Environment

Setting up your home to **manage resources** is important in preventing guarding behaviours. Puppies are naturally curious and often explore their environment, picking up items they should not have or becoming possessive over certain spaces. By **managing their environment**, you can limit their access to valuable items and reduce the chance of guarding developing.

A. Boundaries and Safe Spaces Providing puppies with **safe spaces** where they can enjoy their toys, chews, or food without interruption is key to creating a stress-free environment. Having these boundaries in place helps puppies feel secure and reduces the need to guard.

- **Crates, Pens, and Gated Areas**: Set up crates, pens, or gated areas where puppies can retreat with their resources. This space should be their own where they can chew or rest without the pressure of others taking their items away. Over time, these spaces become **predictable safe zones**, reducing the likelihood of guarding.

B. Rotating High-Value Items Puppies can become attached to certain toys or objects, particularly high-value items like bones or chews. By **rotating** these items and not always leaving them available, you reduce the chance of the puppy becoming overly attached or possessive.

- **Introduce New Toys Gradually**: Instead of leaving all toys out for the puppy to access, introduce them one at a time and rotate them regularly. This keeps the puppy engaged and interested while reducing their potential for **excessive attachment** to any single item.

Encouraging Calmness and Optimism

Teaching puppies how to stay calm in the presence of valued resources can go a long way in preventing guarding behaviours. By building a **positive and optimistic outlook** in your puppy, they learn they do not need to protect their resources because they will not lose them.

A. Enrichment and Calm Activities Enrichment activities, such as **scatter feeding** or scent work, encourage puppies to engage their minds and bodies in a healthy, constructive way. These activities provide mental stimulation while promoting calmness, which helps reduce anxiety around resources.

- **Scatter Feeding**: Instead of feeding from a bowl, scatter kibble or treats around the yard or house and let the puppy find them. This turns mealtime into a game and reduces the sense of needing to guard a bowl.

B. Positive Reinforcement for Calm Behaviour Rewarding puppies for staying calm around valuable items is essential to preventing guarding. When puppies learn that staying calm results in rewards, they are less likely to become defensive or possessive in the future.

- **Reward Calmness**: During play sessions, reward your puppy for sitting calmly or relaxing around toys or other dogs. This reinforces the idea that **calm behaviour** leads to positive outcomes.

Building Trust with Your Puppy

Building trust with your puppy is the foundation of preventing resource guarding. If your puppy knows that you will not take their items away without reason and that good things happen when they share or give up items, they will be far less likely to guard in the future.

A. Avoid Harsh Corrections One of the quickest ways to damage trust with a puppy is through **harsh corrections**. Taking items away forcefully or punishing your puppy for guarding can worsen their behaviour. Instead, focus on **positive reinforcement** and management strategies. Look at the situation and how you can change the "in-the-moment situation" into a positive.

B. Let Your Puppy "Win" When you play games like "Fetch" or "Toy Switch" with your puppy, sometimes let them "win" by keeping the toy. This helps build their confidence and teaches them that they do not always have to give up their resources.

Addressing Guarding Early

If you notice early signs of guarding behaviour in your puppy, it is important to address it **at once**. Resource guarding can spread to more items or situations if not managed early, making it harder to change later. By setting your puppy up for success with **positive experiences** around resources, you can prevent guarding from escalating.

Chapter 5: Preventing Resource Guarding in Puppies

Summary:

- **Early Socialization**: Key to preventing guarding behaviours.
- **Sharing and Trading Games**: Encourage puppies to exchange toys and understand that giving up items is positive.
- **Teach Cues**: Start "drop it" and "leave it" early on for lifelong behaviour benefits.

Checklist:

- Play games that encourage sharing and trading.

- Reinforce positive interactions around food and toys.
- Choose individual spaces in multi-dog homes to prevent competition.

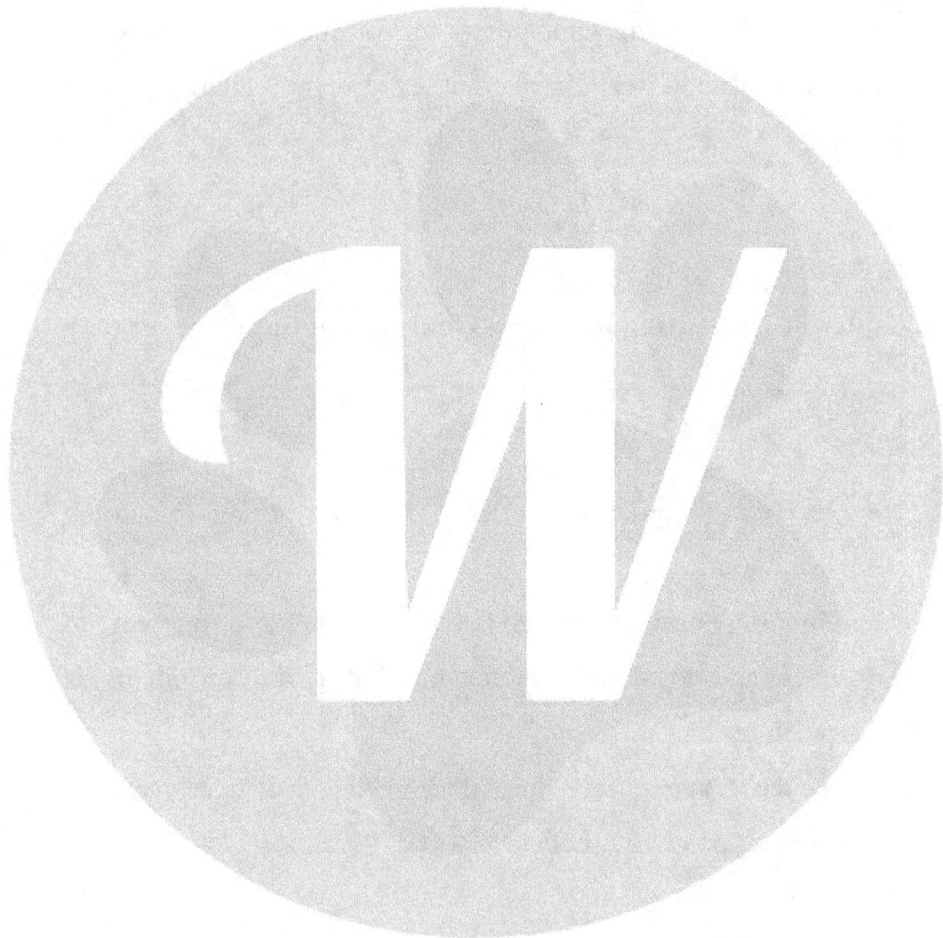

Chapter 6: Managing Resource Guarding in Adult Dogs

This chapter provides practical strategies for managing resource guarding in adult dogs, including behaviour modification, environmental adjustments, and calming techniques.

When resource guarding develops in adult dogs, it is essential to approach the behaviour with a **combination of management and behaviour modification techniques**. While preventing guarding behaviours in puppies is ideal, many dogs develop guarding tendencies as they grow older, and the behaviour can intensify if left unchecked. In this chapter, we will explore practical strategies for **managing and changing resource guarding** in adult dogs, focusing on **positive reinforcement**, environmental management, and ensuring long-term success.

Identifying the Extent of Resource Guarding

Before tackling resource guarding in an adult dog, it is essential to name the **specific triggers** and the extent of the behaviour. Some dogs may only guard a few items, while others may show broader guarding tendencies.

A. What is Your Dog Guarding? The first step is to assess **what** your dog is guarding. Is it food, toys, specific spaces, or found objects? The more items or spaces your dog guards, the more complex the management process becomes.

- **Specific Items**: Some dogs will guard only high-value items, like bones, toys, or food bowls.
- **Spaces**: Others may guard resting spots, such as their bed or crate, and become defensive when someone approaches.
- **Random Items**: In some cases, dogs guard random items they find, like socks or shoes. This is often more unpredictable and can be harder to manage.

B. When Does Resource Guarding Happen? It is also essential to see the **context** in which resource guarding happens. Does the dog only guard certain items around other dogs, or does it happen with humans, too? Are they more likely to guard in certain rooms or times of the day? Understanding the **patterns** of guarding behaviour helps tailor your approach to managing it.

- **Dog-Dog Guarding**: If your dog guards resources from other dogs in the household, this may involve competition for food or attention. In such cases, creating **separate spaces** during feeding times can be helpful.

- **Guarding from Humans**: Dogs who guard items from humans often need to be reconditioned to understand that humans approaching them near their resources is a positive experience.

Behaviour Modification Techniques

Modifying guarding behaviour in adult dogs requires patience and consistency. The goal is to teach your dog that **sharing or giving up resources** leads to positive outcomes. Building trust and reducing stress makes the dog less likely to guard over time.

A. Disengagement and "Leave It" Teaching your dog to **disengage** from the item they guard is an essential part of behaviour modification. When used correctly, the "Leave it" cue encourages the dog to move away from the item without feeling threatened.

- **How to Teach "Leave It"**: Start with a low-value item your dog is less likely to guard. Hold a high-value treat in your hand and say "Leave it" as you present the item. Once the dog disengages from the item (even just by looking away), reward them with the treat. Gradually increase the value of the item being guarded as your dog becomes more comfortable.

B. Teaching "Drop It" for Guarded Items

"Drop it" is one of the most valuable cues for resource guarders. Still, before expecting your dog to drop an item they value, it is essential to **build a positive association** with the word "Drop" through **classical conditioning**. This foundation makes the cue meaningful to your dog before they are asked to relinquish an object.

Classical Conditioning for "Drop It":

This next challenge involves introducing the word "Drop" in a way that makes your dog **excited** about it, using **high-value rewards,** and ensuring the process is fun and rewarding.

How to Begin the Classical Conditioning:

1. **Prepare High-Value Treats**: Boil a piece of chicken breast or use another protein your dog loves. If they cannot tolerate chicken, use their favourite veggie or treat—something that genuinely excites them.
2. **Cut the Treat into Small Pieces**: The size does not matter, but the **value** of the treat is crucial. The higher the value, the more your dog will associate the cue with something positive.

3. **Set Up for Success**: Keep the treats **ready and available** at random times during the day. The idea is to be **unpredictable** when this happens.

4. **Start the Game**: Say "NICE!" thrice a day and **drop three pieces of chicken** in front of your dog. Ensure they **see** you do this and immediately associate the dropped food with something fantastic happening. You are teaching them that "Drop" always leads to something better.

5. **Special Instructions for Multi-Dog Households**: If you have more than one dog, and they squabble over food or treats, practice this **separately** with each dog on their own **station** (mat, bed, etc.). Use baby gates if necessary, and ensure you stay between the stations to manage any competition. If your dogs do not have their own stations yet, train this skill first before moving to this exercise.

Advanced Steps: After conditioning the word, use it in situations where your dog has a low-value item they may give up more easily, such as a toy or object they are not guarding aggressively. Gradually increase the value of the items as the dog builds confidence in the "Drop it" cue.

Adding Handfeeding to Build Predictability and Relationship:

When resource guarding involves the owner, the **conversation of predictability** and trust between the dog and guardian often shifts.

Handfeeding can **rebuild that relationship** and change how your dog views interactions with you around food or resources.

Hand-Feeding Steps:

1. **Start with Kibble**: Begin by using your dog's kibble and **hand-feed** them throughout the day. This is not about holding a handful of food for them to eat from but rather offering single pieces of kibble **for any behaviour** you like.

2. **Capturing Behaviour**: This hand-feeding technique allows you to capture spontaneous behaviours that your dog offers without being asked. If they are lying quietly, for example, walk up to them and place a piece of kibble between their paws to reinforce that **calm behaviour**.

3. **Minimal Bowl Feeding**: While you can still offer some food from a bowl during regular mealtimes, **keep it minimal**. The primary goal is to hand-feed throughout the day to create positive, spontaneous interactions with your dog.

4. **No Reprimands**: In the future, take a holiday from **reprimands, no's, shouting, or aversive tools** like spray bottles, shock collars, or metal collars. These will only inhibit the progress of this plan. The focus is on building a **willing and motivated learner** by reinforcing behaviours you want to see more of rather than punishing the behaviours you do not.

Calmness Protocol (Feed and Leave):

This exercise is about using your dog's daily food allowance to **capture moments of calmness** and reward them.

1. **Observe Calmness**: When your dog is resting calmly or relaxing, drop a piece of **low-value food** nearby without creating any feelings of conflict.

2. **Avoid Conflict**: Do not move toward your dog too purposefully or bend over them in a way that might make them feel pressured to disengage from their relaxing spot. Simply drop the food and walk away, reinforcing the choice to remain calm.

These steps create a **positive foundation** for teaching "Drop It" and can significantly affect how your dog views resource-guarding behaviours, building **trust,** and reinforcing calm, willing behaviour. The hand-feeding activity further enhances predictability, shifting your dog's feeling of food-related interactions with you.

C. Positive Reinforcement for Sharing The key to reducing resource guarding is to **make sharing rewarding**. By using positive reinforcement when your dog voluntarily gives up or shares an item, you teach them that good things happen when they are not guarding.

- **Reinforce Calm Behaviour**: If your dog is calm around a resource or willingly gives up an item, reward them immediately with a treat or praise. This helps build **positive associations** with sharing, making it more likely that the dog will repeat the behaviour in the future.

D. Desensitization and Counterconditioning For dogs with more severe guarding behaviours, a combination of **desensitization and counterconditioning** can help change their emotional response to perceived threats.

- **Desensitization**: Begin by introducing low-level exposure to the triggers that typically cause guarding (such as approaching their food bowl or bed). Start at a distance where the dog does not react and gradually move closer over time, rewarding calm behaviour at each step.
- **Counterconditioning**: Pair the approach to the guarded item with something positive, like a high-value treat. Over time, the dog will begin to associate your approach with good things happening, reducing their need to guard.

E. Disengagement Game

Disengagement games are a powerful tool in resource-guarding modification. They teach the dog to voluntarily move away from or leave an item or area without feeling threatened or forced. These games are particularly useful for dogs that struggle with guarding certain spaces, objects, or even food. The goal is to make disengaging a **fun and rewarding** experience for the dog, helping them feel safe and comfortable with giving up control.

How to Play the Disengagement Game:

Level 1: Unknown Objects in a Safe Environment

- **Step 1**: Start in a low-distraction, familiar environment (like your living room) with an **unknown object** your dog has no history of guarding (e.g., a random household item like a pillow or a cardboard box). Place the item on the floor.
- **Step 2**: Keep your dog on a loose leash to prevent them from interacting too much with the item. As your dog looks at or approaches the object, say "Yes!" or click (if using a clicker) and toss a treat a few feet away from the object.
- **Step 3**: Encourage your dog to move toward the treat. Reward them for **disengaging** from the item.
- **Step 4**: Repeat the process, gradually allowing the dog to interact slightly with the object before disengaging. Over

time, the dog learns that moving away from the object leads to a **positive reward**.

Level 2: Familiar People or Objects Once your dog is comfortable disengaging from unknown items, you can raise the difficulty by introducing **familiar items** or people with no history of guarding.

- **Step 1**: Use an item your dog likes but does not guard (e.g., a toy they play with regularly). Allow your dog to sniff or approach the toy.
- **Step 2**: As they engage with the toy, use the cue "Yes!" or your clicker and toss a treat away from the toy. Encourage your dog to leave the toy and go after the treat.
- **Step 3**: Gradually increase the level of engagement before rewarding disengagement. You can vary the timing of the reward to make the game more dynamic.

Level 3: Random Objects in a New Context Once your dog confidently disengages from familiar items, it is time to try random objects in **unfamiliar locations** where the dog has not shown any guarding behaviour.

- **Step 1**: Take your dog outside to a neutral area like the **front yard** or another space they do not associate with guarding.
- **Step 2**: Place a random item (e.g., a garden glove) on the ground and repeat the disengagement process. Reward your

dog for moving away from the object, ensuring the reward is **more valuable** than the item being guarded.

Level 4: Disengaging from Guarded Objects Once your dog has mastered disengaging from random objects, you can gradually introduce items they have a **history of guarding**. This step must be done slowly and carefully to prevent the dog from becoming anxious or defensive.

- **Step 1**: Begin with a guarded item in a **low-stress environment** where the dog feels safe (e.g., a toy they often guard).
- **Step 2**: Allow your dog to interact with the item, and once they seem relaxed, use the cue "Yes!" and toss a treat away from the object. Reward them for moving away from the guarded item.
- **Step 3**: Over time, increase the difficulty by allowing your dog to engage with the item for longer periods before rewarding disengagement. Always ensure that the reward (high-value treat or praise) is **worth more** than the item being guarded.

Why This Works: Disengagement games teach your dog to **voluntarily move away** from objects they may otherwise guard, turning the experience into a **positive** rather than a defensive one. This game is a powerful behaviour modification tool because it promotes **calmness** and gives the dog a sense of **control** over their choices, reducing the need to guard.

By introducing these games gradually, your dog will learn that leaving an object does not mean losing it forever—on the contrary, it means **better rewards** and **positive experiences**.

Environmental Management Strategies

Managing the dog's environment is essential for preventing resource-guarding triggers from escalating. By structuring the dog's surroundings to reduce competition and stress, you can limit the chances of guarding occurring.

A. Feeding Separately If your dog guards food from other dogs or humans, set up a **separate feeding area** where they can eat without feeling threatened. This could involve using baby gates and crates or feeding the dog in an entirely different room.

- **No-Competition Zones**: In multi-dog households, create **no-competition zones** for feeding and chewing on toys. By giving each dog their own space, you reduce the need for guarding.

B. Use of Barriers, such as baby gates or crates, can help prevent guarding by creating **safe spaces** for your dog to enjoy their resources. These barriers ensure that other dogs or people do not approach while the dog is eating or playing with toys, reducing the chance of guarding behaviour being triggered.

- **Safe Spaces**: Choose certain areas as the dog's safe spaces, where they are not disturbed. These spaces allow the dog to feel secure and limit the need to defend items.

C. Rotating High-Value Items If your dog tends to guard certain high-value items like toys or bones, **rotating** them can help prevent them from becoming overly attached. Remove the guarded item for a while and introduce other toys to keep the dog engaged.

Calming the Stress Bucket

As mentioned earlier, resource guarding can be worsened by a **full-stress bucket**. Addressing underlying stress and anxiety can significantly reduce guarding behaviours.

A. Active Rest and Quiet Time Ensure your dog has plenty of **rest and downtime** in a quiet, safe space. Rest periods help lower stress levels and give the dog time to recover from overstimulation, which can contribute to guarding.

- **Crate or Quiet Room**: Set up a crate or quiet room where your dog can rest undisturbed. Use soft bedding, calming music, or a stuffed Kong to encourage relaxation.

B. Mental Enrichment: Enrichment activities, such as **puzzle toys**, **sniffing games**, and **scent work**, can help reduce stress and provide a positive outlet for your dog's energy. These activities engage the dog's mind and reduce anxiety, which lowers the risk of guarding behaviours.

- **Find It Games**: Playing "Find it" with treats hidden around the house encourages your dog to engage their nose, helping them **disengage from guarding** and focus on the task at hand.

When to Seek Professional Help

If your dog's resource guarding is **severe** or escalating despite your best efforts, it may be time to seek help from a **qualified behaviour consultant**. Professional trainers can provide personalized plans for managing and changing the behaviour, especially when the dog shows aggressive guarding tendencies.

- **Aggression or Biting**: If your dog's resource guarding has escalated to **biting** or causing harm, seeking professional help is critical. A behaviour consultant can assess the situation and develop a safe and effective behaviour modification plan.

Long-Term Management for Success

Managing resource guarding in adult dogs is a long-term training commitment, and consistency is key. By combining **behaviour modification**, **environmental management**, and **positive reinforcement**, you can significantly reduce guarding behaviours and create a more harmonious home environment.

Chapter 6: Managing Resource Guarding in Adult Dogs

Summary:

- **Name Triggers**: Recognize what items or spaces your dog guards.
- **Behaviour Modification Techniques**: Use positive reinforcement and disengagement exercises.
- **Consistency and Patience**: Building trust takes time, so approach training gradually.

Checklist:

- Practice "drop it" and disengagement games.
- Avoid punishment; focus on positive reinforcement.
- Use hand-feeding to build trust and reduce guarding behaviour.

Chapter 7: Addressing Resource Guarding in Rescue Dogs

Many rescue dogs come with an often-unknown history, making their behaviours—including **resource guarding**—more unpredictable and challenging to manage. For dogs that have experienced trauma, abandonment, or inconsistent care, resource guarding can be deeply rooted in **survival instincts**. This chapter will focus on understanding the unique challenges that **rescue dogs** face regarding resource guarding and how to approach these situations with care, patience, and positive reinforcement.

Why Resource Guarding is Common in Rescue Dogs

Resource guarding is a natural survival behaviour that has been passed down through generations of dogs. In a **rescue setting**, this behaviour can be amplified by past experiences such as a lack of consistent access to food, neglect, or competition with other animals for resources.

A. Competition and Deprivation in Early Life Many rescue dogs come from environments where resources—such as food, water, toys, or even safe spaces—were **scarce** or fiercely competed for. Dogs that have had to fight for survival often develop guarding behaviours to ensure they keep access to what little they have.

- **Example**: Dogs rescued from hoarding situations or puppy mills may have been forced to compete for every meal. In these cases, resource guarding can become a well-ingrained behaviour, even in environments where resources are now plentiful.

B. Trauma and Inconsistent Care Rescue dogs often come from backgrounds where they experience **inconsistent care** or even abuse. As a result, their relationship with resources may be tied to **survival and self-preservation**. These dogs may guard because they have learned that resources can be taken away unexpectedly or because they feel insecure about their access to food, space, or affection.

C. Unknown Histories With many rescue dogs, especially those adopted from shelters, much of their history is unknown. You may not know what specific triggers your dog has or how they have been treated in the past. As a result, resource guarding may appear unpredictably as the dog tries to navigate their unfamiliar environment.

Understanding the Needs of Rescue Dogs with Guarding Behaviours

Addressing resource guarding in rescue dogs requires understanding their emotional and psychological needs. The following strategies will help you approach these situations with empathy and **positive reinforcement**, creating an environment of **trust and security**.

A. Building Trust and Predictability Rescue dogs often have trust issues, especially when it comes to their resources. One of the most important steps in managing resource guarding is to build a relationship based on **trust and predictability**. Dogs need to know that you are not a threat to their resources and that good things happen when they interact with you.

- **How to Build Trust**: Avoid forcibly taking items from your dog or punishing guarding behaviour. Instead, teach your dog that when you approach, they will receive something **better** than what they already have. Use high-value treats and positive reinforcement to build positive associations with your presence.

B. Creating a Secure Environment Many rescue dogs have never had a consistent home environment. They may feel overwhelmed by their new surroundings, leading to **anxiety** and increased guarding behaviours. It is crucial to provide a structured, safe environment where they know their needs will be met.

- **Safe Zones**: Create **safe zones** in your home where your dog can relax and enjoy high-value items without feeling threatened. Use crates, pens, or designated rooms where your dog can chew on bones, eat meals, or play with toys without interference.
- **Routine and Structure**: Set up a daily meal, walk, and playtime routine. The predictability of these routines will help reduce anxiety and make your dog feel more secure, leading to less guarding.

Positive Reinforcement Techniques for Resource Guarding in Rescue Dogs

Many rescue dogs are overly sensitive to their environment, and traditional punishment-based training methods can do more harm than good. The key to success with rescue dogs is using **positive reinforcement** techniques to change their behaviour.

A. The Power of Positive Associations To reduce resource guarding, teach your dog that your approach is a **positive experience**. Start by creating small moments of **positive interaction** when your dog has a resource, whether it is food, a toy, or space.

- **Treat Drops**: Approach your dog when they are enjoying a meal or chewing on a toy and toss a high-value treat near them. Over time, this will teach your dog that when you approach, good things happen, and they do not need to guard the resource.

- **Building on Success**: Gradually decrease the distance between you and the resource over time. Start from a distance where your dog is comfortable and slowly move closer, continuing to drop treats as you approach.

B. Teaching "Drop It" with Rescue Dogs For dogs with a history of resource guarding, teaching a dependable **"drop it"** cue can help prevent conflicts over items. Use **classical conditioning** to introduce the word "drop" by pairing it with something of even higher value than the item your dog is guarding.

- **Classical Conditioning Approach**: Say "drop it" and immediately toss a high-value treat or toy. When your dog releases the item, reward them with something better than what they had. This teaches the dog that dropping the item is not a loss but an opportunity for a bigger reward.

- **Gradual Progression**: Start with items of **low value** to your dog and gradually build up to higher-value resources as their confidence and trust in the cue grows.

Managing Resource Guarding in a Multi-Dog Rescue Home

Resource guarding can quickly become a source of conflict for those adopting multiple rescue dogs or integrating a new rescue dog into a home with existing dogs. Special management and training strategies are needed to keep the household peaceful.

A. Separate Feeding and Play Areas Many rescue dogs come from situations where they must compete with other dogs for resources. To reduce the likelihood of guarding, ensure that each dog has their own **designated space** for eating and playing.

- **Feeding Separately**: Feed each dog in their own room, crate, or behind a baby gate. This prevents competition and allows each dog to eat in peace without needing to guard their food from others.
- **Controlled Play Sessions**: Watch play sessions between rescue dogs, especially in the beginning. Overstimulation can lead to **competition over toys**, attention, or space, which can escalate into guarding behaviours. Keep sessions short and supervised.

B. Safe Zones and Personal Space Each dog should have their own **safe zone** where they can retreat and relax without interference.

These safe spaces are essential in multi-dog households, especially for rescue dogs that are more likely to feel insecure.

- **Boundary Training**: Teach each dog to respect the other's personal space. Use **boundary training** techniques to reinforce that good things happen when dogs stay in their designated areas.

Case Studies: Success with Rescue Dogs and Resource Guarding

Including **real-life case studies** can help illustrate how behaviour modification techniques work. Here are a few examples of how resource guarding in rescue dogs has been successfully managed:

A. Case Study 1: Max—the Food Guarder Max was a rescue dog found as a stray and had spent months scavenging for food. When he was adopted, he aggressively guarded his food bowl and would growl if anyone approached. Using a combination of **positive reinforcement** and **routine feeding practices**, his owners gradually reduced his guarding behaviours by teaching him that human presence meant more food, not competition.

B. Case Study 2: Bella, the Toy Guarder Bella was adopted from a shelter and showed significant guarding behaviours over toys. Her new owners worked on **teaching "drop it"** using high-value treats. Over time, Bella learned to associate dropping the toy with receiving a better reward, which reduced her guarding tendencies.

Long-Term Success with Rescue Dogs

Modifying resource-guarding behaviour in rescue dogs takes time, patience, and consistency. By building **trust, confidence, and security**, you help your rescue dog feel less anxious about their resources and more relaxed in their new home. Remember, success with behaviour modification is a journey, and every small improvement is a step towards your rescue dog's healthier and happier life.

Chapter 7: Addressing Resource Guarding in Rescue Dogs

Summary:

- **Understand the Root Causes**: Many rescue dogs guard resources due to past trauma, competition, or deprivation.
- **Build Trust and Predictability**: Use positive reinforcement to create a secure and predictable environment.
- **Safe Zones and Structured Management**: Provide separate feeding areas, safe spaces, and consistent routines to reduce guarding behaviours.

Checklist:

- Establish safe zones for your dog to enjoy high-value items undisturbed.
- Use positive reinforcement (e.g., treat drops) to build trust and reduce guarding tendencies.
- Feed dogs separately in multi-dog households and supervise shared playtime.

Chapter 8: Environmental and Management Strategies for Resource Guarding

While behaviour modification is key to addressing resource guarding, environmental management is equally significant in preventing and reducing guarding behaviours. By setting up your home and daily routines to lower the potential for resource guarding, you can help your dog feel more secure and reduce stress. In this chapter, we will explore practical management techniques to create a safe, predictable, and positive environment for your dog.

Creating Safe Spaces: Gated Communities and Boundaries

One of the most effective ways to manage resource guarding is by providing your dog with designated safe spaces where they can enjoy their food, toys, or chews without the threat of competition or interference. These spaces allow your dog to relax and feel secure in their environment, significantly reducing their need to guard.

A. Crates, Pens, and Gated Areas: Using crates, pens, or baby gates to create gated communities for your dog allows them to enjoy their resources without fear of others taking them. These spaces should be set up in low-traffic areas where your dog can retreat for some downtime.

- **How to Use Gated Areas:** Choose a crate, a pen, or a room as your dog's safe space. When they are eating, chewing on a bone, or playing with a toy, ensure they have access to this space without interruption. Use baby gates to prevent other dogs or children from approaching during these times. This prevents competition and creates a predictable environment where your dog does not feel the need to guard.

B. **Teaching Boundaries**: Boundaries help dogs understand which spaces are theirs and which are shared. Teaching your dog to stay on a mat or in a specific area during certain activities, like eating, is a powerful way to manage resource guarding.

- **Mat Training:** Start by introducing a station mat where your dog can go to eat, chew, or rest. Reward them for staying on the mat and engaging with their resources calmly. Over time, the dog will associate this space with positive experiences, making them less likely to guard.

Feeding and Play Management

Resource guarding often occurs during mealtime or when high-value items like toys are introduced. By managing how and where your dog eats and plays, you can reduce the chance of guarding behaviours escalating.

A. Separate Feeding Areas: In multi-dog households, competition over food is one of the leading triggers for resource guarding. By feeding your dogs in separate spaces, you minimize this competition and help each dog feel secure during meals.

- **No-Competition Feeding**: Feed each dog in a different area, using crates, baby gates, or even separate rooms if needed. This ensures that each dog has their own space to eat in peace without worrying about losing their food to another dog.
- Supervised Mealtimes: If you cannot separate dogs during feeding, supervise meals closely and remove food bowls after the dogs have finished eating. This prevents lingering or guarding over empty bowls.

Managing High-Value Toys and Chews

Certain toys, especially **high-value items** like bones, chews, Kongs, or Toppls, can trigger guarding behaviours. To prevent this, it is important to introduce these items in a **controlled environment** where your dog feels safe and secure.

- **Rotate High-Value Items**: Instead of leaving high-value toys out all the time, rotate them to prevent your dog from becoming overly attached or possessive. Only introduce these items during **supervised play sessions** or when your dog is in their **safe zone**.

- **Safe Zone for Chews and Foraging Toys**: Whenever giving your dog bones, chews, or foraging toys like Kongs or Toppls, always provide them in the dog's **safe zone** (such as their crate, bed, or a gated area). This ensures the dog can enjoy the high-value item without feeling threatened or needing to guard it. The safe zone creates a **predictable, non-competitive space** where your dog can relax and engage with their items.

- **Controlled Playtime**: When your dog plays with a high-value item in their safe zone, ensure the area is free from other pets or potential interruptions. Once they lose interest in the item, remove it to prevent guarding behaviours from resurfacing.

Managing Multi-Dog Homes

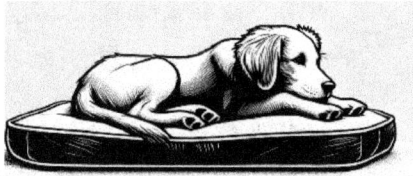

In multi-dog households, managing resource guarding becomes more complex as competition for resources increases. Dogs in these homes often guard food, toys, or even human attention from each other. Setting clear boundaries and providing safe spaces for each dog can reduce tension and guarding behaviour.

A. Individual Spaces for Rest and Enrichment In multi-dog households, it is important that each dog has their own resting space—a crate, bed, or mat where they can relax without interference. This helps each dog feel secure in their space and reduces the need to guard against others.

- **Safe Stations:** Teach each dog to go to their designated station (e.g., a bed or mat) when eating or playing. Use baby gates or crates to create separation when needed, ensuring each dog has a predictable, safe environment.

B. Managing Attention and Affection Competition for human attention can also trigger resource guarding in multi-dog homes. It is important to give each dog individual attention without creating tension or jealousy.

- **Turn-Taking:** Teach your dogs to take turns receiving attention or treats. For example, when one dog is getting affection, the other dog can wait at their station. This reduces competition and teaches patience.

Reducing Triggers and Predictable Approaches

Predictability is key to reducing stress in dogs who guard their resources. You can lower the dog's need to guard against perceived threats by managing your body language, movements, and approaches.

A. **Predictable Approaches to Resources:** Dogs often guard when they feel uncertain about what will happen next. If your approach is predictable and does not pose a threat, your dog will feel more comfortable around their resources.

- **Body Language**: Avoid sudden movements, bending over your dog, or grabbing items quickly. Instead, approach slowly and calmly, giving your dog time to process the situation. When retrieving a guarded item, use a happy tone and engage your dog in a positive game or trade rather than taking the item forcefully.

- **Calm, Controlled Movements:** Practice moving toward your dog's resources in a non-threatening way. Drop treats as you approach to create a positive association with your presence near their guarded item.

- **Avoiding Common Triggers**: Certain actions, like reaching toward a dog's food bowl, moving toward their toys, or getting too close to their resting spot, can trigger guarding behaviour. By avoiding these triggers and giving your dog space, you reduce the chances of guarding escalating.

- **No Reaching or Hovering**: Instead of hovering over your dog or reaching for their food, practice dropping high-value treats from a distance. This teaches your dog that your approach is safe and rewarding.

Long-Term Management and Success

Environmental management is not just a short-term solution but a critical part of long-term success in reducing resource guarding. By consistently using these strategies, you can create a home environment that lowers stress, reduces competition, and fosters positive behaviour.

A. Consistency is Key: Dogs thrive in environments where they understand the rules and boundaries. By consistently managing resources, feeding, and playing, you help your dog feel secure and reduce their need to guard.

B. Adjusting Over Time: As your dog becomes more comfortable with their environment and shows improvement in guarding behaviours, you can begin to adjust your management strategies. Slowly allow more freedom but continue to keep boundaries and supervision as needed to prevent guarding from returning.

Chapter 8: Environmental and Management Strategies

Summary:

- **Safe Spaces**: Create zones where dogs can enjoy resources without disturbance.
- **Reduce Competition**: Use barriers, gates, and separate feeding areas in multi-dog households.
- **Predictability**: Support consistent routines to help your dog feel secure.

Checklist:

- Set up quiet, gated areas for high-value items.
- Maintain consistent feeding and play routines.
- Avoid common triggers like hovering over or reaching for guarded items.

Chapter 9: Building Optimism and Confidence in Dogs

Resource guarding is often rooted in feelings of **insecurity, anxiety, or pessimism**. Dogs that are unsure about their environment or expect negative outcomes are more likely to guard their resources to protect what they have. In this chapter, we will focus on how to **boost your dog's optimism** and build their confidence through **enrichment**, **games**, and relationship-building exercises. By creating a more positive outlook, you can help reduce resource-guarding behaviours and improve your dog's overall emotional state.

The Importance of Optimism in Reducing Resource Guarding

Just like people, dogs can be **optimistic** or **pessimistic**. Dogs that are **pessimistic** are more likely to expect negative outcomes, making them more prone to behaviours like resource guarding. On the other hand, **optimistic dogs** are more confident and secure, expecting good things to happen. When dogs believe they do not need to guard their resources because something better might be coming, they are less likely to show guarding behaviour.

A. What is Optimism in Dogs? Optimism in dogs is the expectation that **positive outcomes** will happen. When dogs feel confident that they will receive something rewarding, they are less likely to feel the need to guard their current resource.

- **Pessimistic Dogs**: These dogs are often more anxious or fearful, expecting negative outcomes. They may guard items more often because they believe they will lose them.
- **Optimistic Dogs**: These dogs are confident and expect good things to happen. They are more likely to share or give up resources because they trust that something better is coming.

B. Why Optimism Matters Building optimism helps dogs feel more **secure** in their environment and reduces the need for guarding.

When dogs know that giving up an item leads to a **positive outcome**, they are less likely to become defensive or possessive.

Confidence-Building Games and Enrichment Activities

Confidence-building games and enrichment activities are essential for fostering **positive emotional states** in dogs. These activities help dogs feel **in control** and teach them that positive experiences happen when they engage with their environment.

A. Optimism Games Optimism games help shift your dog's mindset from defensiveness to confidence and security. These games are designed to be fun, engaging, and low-pressure, helping your dog build trust and positive associations.

- **Toy Switch Game**: This game is a fun way to teach dogs to **relinquish a toy** without feeling that they are losing it. By engaging the dog with two equally valuable toys, you can help them feel excited about switching between toys rather than guarding one.

- **Food Drop**: Teach your dog that dropping an item leads to a reward. Use a **high-value treat** and casually drop it while your dog has a low-value item. Over time, the dog will learn that giving up one thing means getting something even better.

B. Enrichment Activities Enrichment provides mental and physical stimulation, reducing anxiety and **boosting optimism**. These activities help dogs express **natural behaviours** like sniffing, foraging, and problem-solving, which reduce stress and increase emotional well-being.

- **Scent Work and Find It Games**: Engaging your dog's **sense of smell** is one of the best ways to help them feel relaxed and confident. Play "Find It" by hiding treats around the house or yard and encouraging your dog to use their nose to find them. This not only keeps their brain busy but also builds optimism by rewarding them for exploring their environment.
- **Puzzle Toys and Food Dispensing Games**: Use puzzle toys or **food-dispensing toys** like Kongs or Toppls to allow your dog to work for their food. These activities keep their mind engaged and reward them for problem-solving, which boosts confidence and reduces the need to guard food.

Relationship-Building Strategies: Predictability and Trust

Building a strong relationship based on **trust** and **predictability** is key to reducing resource guarding. When dogs trust that their guardians will provide them with what they need and will not lose their resources, they are far less likely to guard.

A. Hand Feeding to Build Trust One of the simplest but most effective ways to build trust is through **hand feeding**. This exercise helps change the conversation between you and your dog around food and resources.

- **How to Hand Feed**: Use your dog's kibble to reinforce behaviours you like during the day. Hand-feed your dog for sitting calmly, lying down, or even engaging in eye contact with you. This process builds a positive association between you and your dog and teaches them that they do not need to guard their resources.
- **Capturing Behaviour**: Handfeeding is also a fantastic way to **capture positive behaviour**. When your dog is relaxed or doing something you like, walk up and give them a piece of kibble. This rewards calmness and encourages your dog to engage in more of the same behaviour.

B. The Importance of Predictability: Predictability is crucial for reducing stress in dogs. When dogs know what to expect, they are less likely to become anxious or feel the need to guard.

- **Routine Feeding and Play**: Setting up predictable **feeding routines** and play sessions helps your dog understand that resources are always available, reducing the need to guard. When your dog knows that mealtime is consistent, they are less likely to feel insecure about food.

- **Clear Communication**: Be clear and consistent in your communication. Use verbal markers like "Yes!" or "Good!" to reinforce positive behaviour. By consistently rewarding your dog for calm and non-guarding behaviour, you build their confidence and help them trust that they will not lose their resources.

Calmness Protocols: Feed and Leave

Calmness protocols are designed to reward **spontaneous moments of calmness**. Teaching your dog that calmness leads to rewards is a powerful way to reduce stress and build optimism.

A. Calmness Protocol (Feed and Leave) This exercise uses your dog's daily food allowance to reward them for being calm and relaxed. By capturing and rewarding these moments, you help reinforce calm behaviour, making it more likely to happen again.

- **How to Use It**: When you observe your dog in a calm state— whether they are lying down, resting, or simply relaxing— drop a **low-value piece of food** nearby and walk away. The key is to be subtle in your approach to avoid interrupting your dog's calmness. This method promotes **calm emotional states** and teaches your dog that being calm leads to positive outcomes.

Creating a Positive Emotional State

Helping your dog achieve a positive emotional state is crucial for reducing guarding behaviour. By creating a **calm, trusting, and predictable environment**, you are teaching your dog that there is no need to guard their resources.

A. Avoiding Negative Triggers Avoid actions that could trigger **anxiety or stress**, such as reaching for their food bowl, grabbing toys suddenly, or using harsh corrections. Instead, focus on **positive reinforcement** and creating a **calm environment** where your dog feels safe.

B. Encouraging Active Rest Encouraging periods of **active rest** can also help calm an anxious or guarding dog. Use **enrichment toys** like Kongs filled with food in your dog's safe zone to create periods of relaxation. This helps them associate rest and calmness with positive outcomes.

Long-Term Strategies for Success

Building optimism and confidence in your dog is not a quick fix but a **long-term strategy** that requires consistency and patience. By consistently rewarding calm, non-guarding behaviour and creating positive experiences around resources, you help your dog feel more secure and less likely to guard.

A. Gradual Progression As your dog becomes more confident and optimistic, you can **gradually** introduce higher-value items and more challenging scenarios. Always watch your dog's emotional state and **adjust as needed** to prevent stress.

B. Reinforcing Success Always reinforce **small victories**— whether it is your dog choosing to walk away from a guarded item or simply relaxing around food. These moments build optimism and create a **positive emotional foundation** for your dog.

Chapter 9: Building Optimism and Confidence

Summary:

- **Optimism**: Dogs that expect positive outcomes are less likely to guard.
- **Confidence-Building Games**: Use enrichment activities to help dogs feel secure and reduce guarding.
- **Routine and Predictability**: Clear routines help dogs understand what to expect, reducing anxiety.

Checklist:

- Engage your dog in enrichment and scent-based games.

- Encourage calm behaviours with a "calmness protocol."

- Build routines that reinforce your dog's sense of security.

Chapter 10: Behaviour Modification Techniques for Resource Guarding

Behaviour modification is a crucial part of addressing and resolving **resource guarding** in dogs. Behaviour modification aims to **replace guarding behaviours** with calm, positive behaviours that help the dog feel more secure and confident. This chapter will cover the core techniques used in behaviour modification, including **classical conditioning**, **positive reinforcement**, and specific **disengagement activities**.

Understanding the Principles of Behaviour Modification

At its core, behaviour modification relies on the idea that **behaviour can be changed** through reinforcement and training. The key to changing resource guarding is teaching the dog that they do not need to guard their items because giving them up results in **positive outcomes**.

Classical Conditioning Classical conditioning involves creating a positive emotional response to a specific stimulus. In the case of resource guarding, this means teaching the dog that the approach of a person (or another dog) while they have a resource results in **good things happening**—like receiving a high-value treat.

- **How It Works**: Every time you approach your dog when they have a guarded item (like a bone or toy), you toss a high-value treat. This creates an association between your approach and something positive. Over time, your dog learns to associate your presence near their resource with rewards rather than the loss of the item.

Desensitization: Desensitization involves exposing the dog to a trigger (e.g., someone reaching towards their guarded item) at a low intensity that doesn't provoke a reaction, then gradually increasing the intensity while maintaining calm behaviour. For resource guarding, this process teaches the dog that the presence or approach of people near their valued resource is not threatening, helping to prevent overreaction and build trust.

- **How It Works:** It involves starting with the trigger (e.g., a person approaching the dog's resource) at a distance or intensity that doesn't provoke guarding behaviour. Over time, the trigger is gradually brought closer or made more intense while ensuring the dog remains calm and relaxed. By pairing this controlled exposure with positive reinforcement, the dog's emotional response shifts (classical conditioning), reducing their need to guard and build confidence in their environment.

Capturing: Capturing is a powerful tool for reinforcing naturally occurring behaviours.

- **How It Works:** It works by marking and rewarding behaviours you want to see more of. For instance, by stepping away from a guarded resource, you can teach the dog to offer those behaviours voluntarily. In resource guarding, capturing moments of disengagement or calmness helps replace guarding behaviours with desirable alternatives, building a foundation for trust and cooperation.

Positive Reinforcement Positive reinforcement involves rewarding your dog for **desired behaviours**—in this case, relinquishing control of a resource. This method teaches your dog that giving up an item or allowing you near a resource is always followed by something they value, like treats or praise.

- **Reward-Based Systems**: Instead of focusing on punishing guarding behaviour, you will focus on **rewarding the behaviour you want**. For example, if your dog willingly walks away from a toy, they usually guard and immediately reinforce this with a treat or affection.

Teaching the "Drop It" Cue

The "Drop It" cue is a critical tool in managing resource guarding, as it encourages your dog to **voluntarily relinquish** an item. This cue is best taught through positive reinforcement and classical conditioning.

A. Classical Conditioning with "Drop It" As described in **Chapter 5**, classical conditioning teaches the dog that the word "drop" is always followed by a **high-value reward**. You will first introduce the cue in low-stress situations so your dog does not need to guard the item.

- **Step-by-Step**: Boil a piece of chicken or use another favourite treat. Say "Drop!" and then drop three pieces of the treat on the floor. Repeat this exercise several times a day in different contexts to build a **positive association** with the word "Drop."

B. Handfeeding and Capturing Calm Behaviour: To build trust, you can incorporate **handfeeding** into your daily routine. When your dog offers calm behaviour, such as lying down or relaxing, reward them with a piece of kibble or their daily food allowance. This reinforces **calm, non-guarding behaviour**.

Disengagement Activities

Disengagement activities are designed to teach your dog to **voluntarily move away** from items they may be inclined to guard. These activities focus on building the dog's confidence and showing them that moving away from an item is **rewarding**.

A. The Disengagement Game: The disengagement game involves teaching your dog that **moving away** from an object or resource results in a reward. This game can be scaled from low to high difficulty, depending on what your dog is comfortable with.

Level 1: Unknown Objects

- Start by introducing a **non-guarded item**, like a pillow or cardboard box. When your dog approaches or looks at the object, say "Yes!" and toss a treat away from the item. This encourages your dog to disengage from the object and go after the treat.
- Repeat several times to build the habit of **voluntarily disengaging** from an object.

Level 2: Familiar Objects

- Use a familiar object your dog does not typically guard (like a toy). As your dog engages with the toy, toss a treat and encourage them to move away from the object to get the treat.

Level 3: Gradual Introduction of Guarded Objects

- Once your dog is comfortable disengaging from non-guarded items, you can begin introducing objects they may guard, such as a favourite toy or bone. Begin in a controlled, low-stress environment and **reward disengagement** with a higher-value treat.

B. The "Find It" Game Another helpful disengagement game is the **Find It** game, which encourages your dog to **focus on their nose** rather than their guarding tendencies. In this game, you hide treats around the room and ask your dog to search for them.

- **How It Works**: Start by tossing a treat on the ground and saying, "Find it!" Allow your dog to use their nose to search for the treat. This game is particularly effective in redirecting your dog's focus from guarding behaviour to a more positive and mentally stimulating activity.

Calmness Protocols

Calmness protocols aim to reward **spontaneous moments of calmness** and encourage your dog to keep a relaxed state, especially around high-value resources.

A. Feed and Leave This exercise involves using your dog's food allowance to reward them for being calm. When your dog is resting or relaxed, drop a low-value piece of food nearby and **walk away** without disturbing them. This reinforces calm behaviour and shows your dog that **relaxation is rewarding**.

- **How It Helps**: Over time, your dog will begin to associate calmness with positive outcomes, which can help reduce the anxiety or insecurity that leads to resource guarding.

Gradual Desensitization

Desensitization involves **slowly and carefully** introducing your dog to situations where they might guard, but in a way that reduces their emotional response over time. This process should be done gradually, ensuring your dog stays calm and **does not feel threatened**.

A. Controlled Exposure For desensitization to work, it is important to begin with low-intensity scenarios. For example, if your dog guards food, start by **walking past** them while they are eating, tossing a treat as you pass to create a positive association. Gradually build up to being closer to them without triggering a guarding response.

- **Slow Progression**: Move slowly through these stages, ensuring your dog is comfortable at each step before increasing the intensity. Rushing this process can lead to setbacks, so it is important to take things **one step at a time**.

Reducing Guarding Through Enrichment

Enrichment activities keep your dog's brain engaged and help reduce the **anxiety** and **boredom** that often contribute to resource guarding. By providing mental stimulation, you can reduce stress and promote a more relaxed state of mind.

A. Scent Work and Puzzle Toys Activities like scent work and puzzle toys allow your dog to engage in **species-typical behaviours** like foraging and problem-solving. This type of enrichment not only satisfies their natural instincts but also helps alleviate boredom and frustration, two common triggers for guarding.

- **Interactive Toys**: Use toys like Kongs or food-dispensing puzzles to keep your dog busy while also providing a rewarding activity that does not involve guarding.

Tailoring Behaviour Modification to Your Dog

While these behaviour modification techniques are effective for many dogs, it is important to tailor your approach to your dog's **individual needs**. Factors like age, breed, and temperament all play a role in how quickly a dog responds to training.

A. Consulting a Professional If your dog's resource guarding is severe, or if you are struggling to make progress, it is important to consult with a professional behaviourist or trainer. They can help you develop a tailored behaviour modification plan that addresses your dog's specific challenges.

Long-Term Success and Consistency

Behaviour modification is not a quick fix; it requires **time, patience, and consistency**. By consistently reinforcing positive behaviours and managing the environment, you can help your dog overcome resource guarding and live a calmer, more secure life.

A. Celebrate Small Wins Every time your dog chooses to **disengage** from a resource, responds to the "Drop It" cue, or stays calm when approached, it is a win. These small victories add up over time and lead to long-term success.

Chapter 10: Behaviour Modification Techniques

Summary:

- **Classical Conditioning**: Use positive associations to change your dog's response to guarded items.
- **Positive Reinforcement**: Reward non-guarding behaviour to encourage calm responses around resources.
- **Disengagement Activities**: Teach your dog to voluntarily move away from guarded items.

Checklist:

- Practice "drop it" with high-value treats as rewards.
- Reinforce calm, non-guarding behaviour with praise or treats.
- Use disengagement games to teach your dog to release resources willingly.

Chapter 11: Managing Multi-Dog Households

Living in a **multi-dog household** comes with its own set of challenges, and resource guarding is one of the most common issues when several dogs share a space. Whether it is guarding food, toys, or even human attention, resource guarding can create tension between dogs and lead to conflicts. This chapter will focus on **proactively managing** multi-dog households to prevent or minimize resource-guarding behaviours and ensure a harmonious living environment.

Understanding the Dynamics in Multi-Dog Homes

Dogs living together naturally form a social hierarchy, but this hierarchy is often fluid, shifting depending on context, available resources, and individual relationships. This fluidity is particularly noticeable in related dogs, such as siblings or parent-offspring pairs, where shared genetics and upbringing can create unique dynamics. Resource guarding can become a **learned behaviour** in multi-dog homes, especially if dogs frequently compete for the same items or space. Understanding and observing these ever-changing dynamics is essential to managing resource guarding effectively. Structured routines, clear boundaries, and proactive training can help reduce tension and foster harmonious interactions.

Competition for Resources In multi-dog households, competition for food, toys, or attention can often trigger guarding behaviours. Some dogs may feel the need to **protect their resources** from other dogs to ensure they have access to them.

- **Why it Happens**: Dogs that feel insecure about their access to resources may become possessive over items, especially in homes where competition is high. Dogs naturally more anxious or lower in the social hierarchy may be more prone to guarding to protect what they feel is theirs.

Recognizing Signs of Guarding In a multi-dog household, it is essential to recognize the early signs of resource guarding before it escalates into a severe problem. Some dogs may begin guarding subtly by stiffening their body posture, growling, or moving between another dog and a resource.

- **Subtle Signs**: Blocking access to food or toys, giving another dog a "hard stare," or even **quietly hovering** near a resource are signs that one dog may be guarding against another. These behaviours can escalate to more aggressive actions like growling, snapping, or lunging if left unaddressed.

Factors That Influence Resource Guarding in Multi-Dog Households

Several factors, including **age differences, size disparities, health conditions, and stress factors,** can influence resource guarding in a multi-dog home. Understanding how these dynamics play a role can help you prevent or manage guarding behaviours more effectively.

Age Differences: Puppies, Adolescents, and Senior Dogs

- **Puppies**: Younger dogs often do not understand **boundaries** and may steal toys or food from older dogs. This can lead to frustration in senior dogs, who are less tolerant of such behaviour.
- **Senior Dogs**: Older dogs may become more **irritable** due to physical discomfort or cognitive decline. They are less likely to tolerate younger dogs' lack of boundaries and may become defensive over their space or resources.
- **Adolescent Dogs**: Adolescents are naturally more inclined to **test limits** and challenge the established hierarchy, which can cause tension and lead to guarding behaviours as they figure out their place in the social structure.

Size Differences: Large vs. Small Dogs

- Size disparities can create **power imbalances**, where larger dogs might physically dominate resources, leaving smaller dogs needing to guard what they have. Conversely, smaller dogs may guard out of a sense of **vulnerability**, especially if they feel they cannot compete physically.

Health Status:

- **Healthy Dogs**: In multi-dog households, healthier dogs may guard resources to **maintain their advantage** over weaker or injured dogs. If resources are perceived as limited, even the healthiest dog may guard more aggressively.
- **Sick or Injured Dogs**: Dogs that are ill or injured may become more **protective** of resources due to their vulnerable state. This heightened guarding behaviour is often a defence mechanism to ensure they have what they need to recover.

Behavioural Dynamics and Stress Factors

- **Stealing and Hoarding**: Some dogs, especially in multi-dog homes, may start stealing toys or food, which can quickly escalate into **guarding behaviours** as competition increases.
- **New Additions to the Household**: The introduction of a **new dog** can disrupt established routines and hierarchies, leading to increased stress and resource guarding as dogs try to adjust to the new social dynamics.
- **Crowded Living Spaces**: Limited space in a home can increase competition for resources and heighten guarding behaviours. Dogs need **personal space** to feel secure, and

the absence of these spaces can make them more likely to guard.

- **Lack of Safe Stations**: Providing each dog with a safe space, such as a crate or bed, is essential. Dogs are more likely to feel insecure without these safe stations, leading to guarding behaviours.

Monitoring Play and Managing Overstimulation

- **Play Dynamics**: Even friendly play between dogs can become guarding if one dog becomes **overstimulated**. Monitoring these interactions is key to ensuring that play does not escalate into competition for toys or human attention.
- **Creating Breaks**: Regular breaks during play help dogs to calm down and prevent overstimulation. This is particularly important in multi-dog households where excitement can quickly lead to **conflict** and guarding.

Managing Resources to Prevent Guarding

The best way to prevent resource guarding in multi-dog homes is through **management**. By setting up the environment in a way that **minimizes competition**, you reduce the likelihood of dogs feeling the need to guard their resources.

Separate Feeding Areas Competition over food is one of the most common triggers for resource guarding in multi-dog homes. Feeding dogs in **separate areas** helps end this competition and allows each dog to feel secure during mealtimes.

- **How to Set It Up**: Feed each dog in their **designated area**, such as a crate, separate room, or behind a baby gate. This ensures that each dog has their own space to eat without feeling pressured or threatened by the presence of other dogs.

Safe Zones for High-Value Items Dogs are more likely to guard **high-value items** like bones, chews, or special toys. Providing each dog with their own safe zone, where they can enjoy these items without interference, reduces the chances of guarding behaviours.

- **Safe Zone Setup**: Choose individual crates, beds, or quiet areas for each dog to enjoy high-value items. This not only prevents competition but also teaches each dog to **relax** and enjoy its resources in its own space.

Controlled Play and Toy Rotation Managing play sessions and rotating toys can prevent dogs from becoming possessive over specific items. Keeping playtime **supervised** ensures that competition does not escalate into guarding or conflict.

- **Toy Rotation**: Instead of leaving toys out all the time, **rotate high-value toys** to keep things fresh and exciting. This prevents dogs from developing a strong attachment to specific items, reducing the likelihood of guarding.

Teaching Turn-Taking and Boundaries

Teaching your dogs to **take turns** with resources, toys, and even attention is a powerful way to reduce guarding behaviours in multi-dog households. It helps each dog understand that waiting their turn will be rewarded, which builds **trust and patience**.

The Power of Turn-Taking Teaching dogs to take turns, especially when receiving attention or playing with toys, helps prevent competition. This method teaches dogs that **good things happen** when they wait for their turn, reducing tension and the likelihood of guarding.

- **How to Teach It**: Start by asking one dog to wait on their station or bed while the other dog receives attention or plays with a toy. Once the first dog is settled, switch and reward the waiting dog. This helps each dog understand that **patience is rewarded**.

Boundary Training Teaching dogs about **personal boundaries** helps prevent competition over spaces like beds or resting areas. Dogs with their designated spot are less likely to feel threatened by the presence of another dog in that space.

- **Mat Training**: Use a station or mat for each dog and reward them for going to their mat and staying there. Over time, dogs will learn to associate their station with **positive experiences** and feel less need to compete for shared spaces.

Managing Human Attention in Multi-Dog Homes

In multi-dog households, dogs may not only guard resources like food or toys but also **human attention**. Some dogs become possessive of their owner's attention, which can lead to tension or even fights with other dogs.

Structured Attention Time To prevent dogs from feeling the need to guard human attention, create **structured time** for each dog to receive individual attention. This helps reduce competition and ensures that each dog feels secure in their bond with their human.

- **One-on-One Time**: Spend time individually with each dog, either through play, training, or quiet bonding time. This helps each dog feel **secure** in their relationship with their human and reduces the desire to compete for attention.

Attention Redirection If you notice one dog starting to guard your attention, use **positive reinforcement** to redirect their focus to more appropriate behaviour. For example, ask the guarding dog to go to their mat or station and reward them for complying. This teaches them that **waiting patiently** is rewarded rather than guarding.

Gradually Introducing New Dogs

Introducing a **new dog** into a multi-dog household can often trigger resource guarding in the resident dog. The stress of a new addition, combined with the potential competition for resources, can lead to tension and guarding behaviours.

A. Slow Introductions New dogs should be introduced to the household **gradually** and in neutral environments whenever possible. This reduces the initial tension and allows the resident dog to adjust to the new presence without feeling threatened.

- **Controlled Interaction**: Use **supervised, short interactions** between the new and resident dogs. Provide plenty of positive reinforcement for calm behaviour and use management tools like baby gates or crates to give the dogs **space** when needed.

B. Managing High-Value Resources During the introduction phase, keep high-value resources like toys, bones, and food out of the equation to reduce the potential for guarding. Allow the dogs to **gradually** adjust to each other before reintroducing these items in a controlled setting.

Long-Term Management and Success

Managing a multi-dog household requires consistent effort and **ongoing management**. You can significantly reduce the likelihood of resource guarding by creating a home environment where competition is minimized, and each dog feels secure in their access to resources.

Consistency and Predictability Dogs in multi-dog households thrive in environments where the **rules are clear** and predictable. Maintaining consistent boundaries, feeding schedules, and routines helps prevent tension and guarding behaviours.

Ongoing Monitoring Even if resource-guarding behaviours diminish, watching interactions and reinforcing positive behaviours is important. This ongoing attention helps keep a harmonious household where all dogs feel safe and secure. Understand the when, where, what (triggers are important to note), and why should always be a consideration when living in a multi-dog household.

Case Study 2: Resource Guarding in a Livestock Guardian Breed

Background:

A six-month-old male, which we will call the L livestock guarding breed, was recently adopted into a farm property. The owner called about resource-guarding behaviours. The owners, experienced with livestock guarding breeds, had two other dogs:

1. An older female, physically failing 13-year-old Livestock Guarding x.
2. An eight-year-old male Livestock Guarding x.

The new dog's history revealed he came from a breeder where the dogs were kept outdoors. Three days before his rehoming, his favourite littermate had been placed into another home, and the breeder observed that he was looking for him. The new dog had then endured a 10–12-hour drive to his new environment. This transition, combined with his adolescent age, likely filled his stress bucket, exacerbating behavioural challenges.

Presenting Problem:

The owners contacted me after a resource guarding incident between the six-month-old and the eight-year-old male. During a shared mealtime indoors, the older male approached the younger dog's bowl, triggering an aggressive response. Outside, the dogs coexisted well and could be walked together without issues, but indoors became a problematic "trigger picture."

Key Observations and Challenges:

- **Stress Factors:** The dog's recent transitions and adolescence contributed to a heightened stress state.
- **Trigger Picture:** Resource guarding was isolated to the indoors, which is where it was initiated.
- **Environmental Preference:** All the dogs preferred lying on ceramic floors over using beds, making station-based strategies less effective. Instead, we did focus on consistent locations. Although, the new dog did not mind the mat at the front door.

- **Rest Deficiency:** The new dog was not receiving adequate rest for his age, further depleting his self-regulating ability.

Management and Training Plan:

1. **Environmental Management:**
   - Installed a large baby gate to separate the dogs during mealtime.
   - Covered the gate with sheets to block visual stimuli.
   - Designated the front entrance (with a large carpet) as the young dog's **safe zone** to build value and predictability in that area.
2. **Stress Reduction:**
   - Introduced passive calming activities to lower the dog's stress bucket. Paired much of the passive calming near the gate to create a conditioning effect.
   - Encouraged quiet, restful periods in the basement, where one of the owners worked remotely. This setup ensured the dog could have undisturbed rest.
3. **Training Exercises:**
   - Used disengagement games to help the young dog manage his emotional responses. For example, practicing with the eight-year-old male on the opposite side of the gate builds tolerance and calmness, as well as creates predictability for the dogs in their safe spaces.

- o Initiating opportunities for the dogs to use their thinking brain.
- o Reinforced the use of the front-door mat as a predictable, safe retreat.

4. **Adjusting for Breed Preferences:**
   - o Avoided station-based strategies due to the dog's preference for the ceramic floor. Instead, focus on building trust and comfort in the chosen safe zone (mat near the door).

5. **Protect the resident dog:**
   - o We made sure the 8-year-old dog was receiving much of the same training and passive calming activities so that the owners could protect him from getting stressed and reacting to the newcomer.

Progress:

By the third session:

- L's stress bucket began to empty, reducing the intensity of his reactions when the 8-year-old door was near the baby gate.
- The young dog began to self-regulate, retreating to his mat near the front door during moments of frustration or overwhelm.
- Both dogs remained separated indoors during meals, preventing further conflict.

- Outside interactions continued without issue, reinforcing the value of outdoor spaces for positive engagement.

Outcome:

The owners were satisfied with the progress over several weeks. They appreciated the practical skills and strategies provided, which they could continue to build upon independently. With management, stress reduction, and a clear, safe zone, the new dog's behaviour inside the home improved significantly, fostering predictability and trust between the dogs.

Key Takeaways for Trainers and Guardians:

1. **Stress Bucket Awareness:** Adolescence, rehoming, long travel, and the loss of a littermate can fill a dog's stress bucket, heightening guarding behaviours. It's important to consider the multi-dog stress bucket dynamic as well.

2. **Trigger Pictures:** Resource guarding can often be context-specific; identifying the trigger picture is key to understanding and working towards resolving the issue.

3. **Breed-Specific Considerations:** Livestock-guarding breeds may not respond well to traditional station-based strategies (often too stressful). Adjustments like ceramic floor safe zones and then focusing on passive calming activities are often more effective.

4. **Self-Regulation:** Training dogs to seek a predictable safe zone during moments of stress can significantly improve behaviour. Building disengagement concepts is a key component to their success.

5. **Rest Matters:** Ensuring adequate rest is critical, particularly for adolescent dogs coping with high stress or new environments.

Chapter 11: Managing Multi-Dog Households

Summary:

- **Challenges in Multi-Dog Homes**: Multi-dog households introduce social dynamics that may increase resource guarding, especially with food, toys, or attention.
- **Social Hierarchy**: Dogs may naturally form a hierarchy, influencing their interactions over shared resources.
- **Managing Resources**: Separate feeding areas, structured turn-taking, and designated rest spaces can reduce competition and promote harmony.

Checklist:

- Establish separate feeding and play areas.

- Encourage turn-taking for resources and attention.
- Use boundaries like mats or stations to prevent tension over spaces.